T0353713

Comments about Dawn Dayton from friends and acquaintances:

Dawn is the smartest, funniest person I know with such a great sense of humor. Of all the people I have worked with through my career, Dawn will be someone I will never forget.

> Andrea Stevens
> Vice President of Business Development
> Amedisys Home Health

Dawn was born to an openminded father, who loved the outdoors and people. Her mother was city born and artistic. At the beginning of World War II, her father became the superintendent of beautiful Brown County State Park in Indiana. The Mead children in their early years grew up there in that wonderful environment and were nourished by it. Later the family developed a flourishing recreational area in the rugged Apalachicola National Forest in the Florida panhandle.

> Anna Altic
> Realtor, Nashville, Tennessee

Dawn's relatable storytelling will have you leaning in to hear all the details. While delighting in her stories, you will have an awareness you are learning a heartwarming lesson.

> Cheryl Thompson, Family Friend

Dawn is a good story tell, funny even when she doesn't mean to be. She is intelligent and quick witted.

> Caris Porter, Family Friend

As Dawn's husband, I have reads Dawn's writing for many years. She is informative and entertaining. She worked for an HCA hospital and authored their monthly newsletters as well as another for a Senior's organization sponsored by the hospital. I encourage you to give yourself the pleasure of reading her book, *Roughing It*.

> Bill Dayton
> Retired NASA Engineer

I have known Dawn, from my youth in Florida. She was always independent and full of adventurous ideas.

Janet Bargo. Family Friend

I want to thank Dawn for sharing her story with me. It was an interesting, heartwarming, and humorous real life adventure.

Stacy Barnes, Family Friend

Dawn has beautifully expressed her memories of her life in a different time. Love how she weaves some humor into her story. Really enjoyed the read.

Kathy Mead, A reader

Dawn is a knowledgeable woman, yet is difficult to describe. On the outside she is the typical grandmother with a warm smile and loving eyes. In truth, she is anything but typical. He witty, authentic personality and amusing stories make her one of a kind.

Annie Altic

Dawn is a great, detailed story teller. Her life story is fascinating. Dawn shares the truth about her life.

Valerie Jenkins, Family Friend

Dawn is a sharp, quick. Fearless lady, who has many memories of a well-lived life. Her wonderful stories are a privilege to hear and to enjoy what was. She is also an avid reader.

Cecillia Watson, A Friend

ROUGHING IT

M DAWN DAYTON

authorHOUSE®

AuthorHouse™
1663 Liberty Drive
Bloomington, IN 47403
www.authorhouse.com
Phone: 833-262-8899

Published by AuthorHouse 02/11/2025

ISBN: 979-8-8230-3961-1 (sc)
ISBN: 979-8-8230-3962-8 (hc)
ISBN: 979-8-8230-3960-4 (e)

Library of Congress Control Number: 2024926112

Print information available on the last page.

CONTENTS

I dedicate this book to my older brother Byron who always behave as older brother should.

FAMILY HISTORY

M Y BROTHER AND I have lived close to a century now, the last of our family of six. What I think of as "back home", is a silver lake deep in the Apalachicola National Forest in north Florida beginning in the 1950's. That Florida wouldn't be recognizable to the folks who live or travel there or to the beaches, condominiums and Disney World now. We had the beaches, and animal parks, but it was not so commercialized, thus it was very different. Our adventures weren't man-made or artificial. We didn't stare at an alligator from a distance; we swam with them. Our beaches had scattered cottages, sea shells in abundance and no McDonalds to grab a quick lunch. The beautiful springs and virgin forests were in state parks and forests, but not with all kinds of caution signs and gift shops. Our home place at Silver Lake was one big adventure on a daily basis, and we, the gators, other varmints and the public had a mutual respect. There was so much that was still virgin. We did not think of it as an adventure; It was our modern-day life. We were just making a living there. There, at Silver Lake, where our one big story takes place, though we did have our beginning in another "world" entirely.

Much to our regret now, neither our father nor mother

talked much about their early lives. I have relied on my brother Byron's recollections and Mother's scrapbook for our first few years. I so regret we didn't press them to tell their stories. My brother and I compiled this information by surmising. We do know our dad was born in 1899 in Indianapolis, Indiana, the third of five children by Charles and Tillie Mead.

Charles Mead built factories. and during his career, he built in built in Indianapolis, Indiana, Chicago, Illinois and Poughkeepsie, New York. One factory was for Westinghouse,that manufactured light bulbs. From the genealogy we have, the dates indicate that some of his children were born in Chicago, where Tillie died in 1909 leaving behind five children, the youngest about, three years old. After the death of their mother, Charles left Chicago, to further his career in Poughkeepsie, New York. Apparently, as he traveled for work, his young children were left in the care of their grandparents on a farm in Indiana. If that is the way it happened, it must have been quite an undertaking for those grandparents. While in Poughkeepsie, Charles died of pneumonia. It's interesting to note here that the man that built factories now has a great grandson, Douglas Mead, who builds factories in Florida.

Dad left the farm at age sixteen to join his father in Poughkeepsie, where he studied engineering. He moved to Chicago, and was employed by the DeLavel Corporation, that holds the patent on the first vacuum operated milking machine that our father, Hansel Mead designed. At the beginning of WWII, Hansel left there with his family to work in Indianapolis at Allison Aircraft. He was working on a secret project (the super-charger for the P-38 airplane). While employed there he set his family on a farm down in Brown County, forty-five miles south near Nashville.

Mother was born in 1909 in Chicago. She was schooled in there and graduated from the Chicago Art Institute. She was an artist with an artistic temperament and tastes, a well-read, and interesting lady. She was not as out-going as our dad, being reserved, yet through the years she was a true partner in every way. She was an empathetic person and was frequently helping needy persons, young and old.

Her father, Frank Tracy, came to Chicago from Iowa, where his parents were Irish immigrants. He was a prominent dentist in Blue Island, Illinois. At the time he was a dentist, X-rays were just beginning to be used and proper precautions were not understood or observed. He apparently took the X-rays by holding the patients mouth open with his thumb. I check on-line for an image of these early x-ray machines and beside the image of one was the text that read: "Going to the dentist in 1909, was a nightmare,"

Early X-ray machine. "Going to the dentist in 1909, was a Nightmare."

meaning for the patient, however could also be for the dentist. Each time my grandfather came to visit, he would check our teeth. There was some discussion amongst us over Grandpa's thumb. Where there was supposed to be a thumb nail, was a strange waxy looking substance like yellowish, chewed bubblegum, instead of a nail. That thumb looked foul and we didn't want it near our mouths. He attempted to create his own nail and tape it on, but it didn't fool us. Did it arouse consternation among his patients? Perhaps his charm and self-confidence could serve as a camouflage in itself. We'll never know.

While the infection was still localized, he did not attribute its state to the X-ray machine. We now understand that the X-ray machine was the cause later for his horrible death to skin cancer. Starting in that thumb, by the time of his death, the cancer had progressed all down his arm and the side of his body.

Mother's natural mother named, Theresa Sweitzer was born 1882 from immigrant, German, parentage. Byron remembers, our granny speaking only in German when talking with him, although that was before I was born. When she lived with us during her later years, I remember her cooking German treats like Kuchen, making sure that we pronounced the dishes correctly. She was a cellist who played in the orchestra pits of the silent movies and in posh restaurants in Chicago. We have a photo of her when a young woman. She was very attractive in a long dress with thick hair arranged in a bouffant on top of her head. She wore lots of jewelry. In the photo she's posed with her cello. Mother once told me that when she was little, if Granny had to play at night, she would be put to bed in the cello case.

Granny had a big personality, but was not the warm, cuddly person one associates with a granny. As she got older, the slender body became downright chubby. Under the finery she always wore a full-torso girdle, summer and winter, that felt like stiff body armor. She lived with us the last few years of her life. Overweight and grumpy, she dished out shame and criticism, so we tended to keep our distance. Interestingly, she and Dad got along fine. He would josh with her and she would sass him back.

Mother's mother and father were divorced and he remarried a refined, gentle lady from a posh family, named Queenie. That name was so apt, as she had a queenly presence. She was a tiny, warm lady, delicate in appearance, and soft spoken. We all admired and loved her. We were always eager to visit Grandpa and Queenie and have them visit us. So much of mother's character, stemmed from the close relationship she had with Queenie. Queenie was one of the early Jehovah's Witnesses in the Chicago area and was an avid student of the Bible. According to Byron, during the great depression she was always taking care of stray animals and would even feed the hungry homeless men that came by from the railroad yard. Mother was very loyal to her mother, but it seemed as a daughter, she was closer to her step-mother, Queenie.

Queenie's father, Mr. Eddy had a workshop in his basement where he made stained glass windows for churches. Also he owned houses he rented out and had other real estate holdings, including the house Grandpa and Queenie lived in. When Mr. Eddy died, Queenie inherited all these holdings. The Eddys were also rich in books and music as well, because Mother inherited some of those things after Queenie died.

I don't think that Grandpa was good husband material, because when Queenie was dying of kidney disease, she came down to our small home in Florida for Mother to care for her. When Queenie died, it shocked everyone concerned, that she left her entire estate to Mother, and that included the home in Blue Island, that Grandpa and Queenie were living in. Byron accompanied his mother to Blue Island, where the inheritance was being settled. It was very disturbing for him, because there were terrible arguments between Mother and her father and brother. Mother ended the dissension by turning the entire inheritance over to her father. However that compromise stipulated that when he made a will, a portion of the estate should be bequeathed to Queenie's niece; That had been Queenie's original wishes. After Grandpa died, she had to go back to Blue Island again, to see to it that Queenie's wishes were fulfilled concerning the niece. This put her in opposition to her brother Bob, who then was the inheritor. This move was entirely at the expense of Mother. Byron's recollection is that although she turned Queenie's inheritance over to them, it seems, that they continued holding a grudge. At that time, we were getting a new start, living in a tiny unfinished pine house outside Tallahassee, Florida. We certainly could have used the money.

Mother often stated, "You don't really know anyone, even your family, until there is a death." That was the most I ever heard her speak of it. Such was her decency, that even Byron, who traveled with her never knew any details of her father and brother's treachery. Furthermore, she refrained from exposing her father and brother's bullying to the rest of us kids. I never knew the particulars of the legacy, until very recently. The worst of that affair was that they stayed angry with Mother ever after. In my child's mind, I actually thought their anger stemmed from being big city people. All the country people we encountered and associated with were fine people in my mind, however my reasoning might not have been too far off. She would not lower herself to squabble over material things.

When Mother died, she had in her possession many books that had been in Queenie's family. Now some of these are captive with me for my enjoyment. In addition to fine books, was a Gibson guitar, and a violin. My brothers and sister bent over backwards to be accommodating to one another after Mother's death.

Years before the wretched business with the legacy,

Mother's brother Bob, married with three children, came to visit us in Indiana. We never got to spend much time with them after this particular visit, which meant no further association with first cousins for the rest of our lives. That was all because of a dog.

In their car, was his wife, three children, and his beloved pet, a Great Dane dog named Fritz. One gets the impression that Uncle Bob was a bit arrogant. That large dog dominating the car with small children reveals a lot. Now Fritz was most definitely a city, in-house dog. Great Danes are sometimes described as a mastiff type with *elegance.* One of their characteristics is they tend to bloat and be gassy. Descriptive words like mastiff, bloat, drool, does not conjure elegance in my mind, although the Great Danes do have good dispositions. His height may have been anywhere around thirty two to thirty five inches and weight, 110 to 150 pounds. That height allowed him to place his huge jowls on the dinner table and roll his eyes imploringly at Bob -- he most assuredly slobbered. Another characteristic of this large dog, is they are very insecure about being alone.

It should be noted that there is no small difference between a city animal lover and a farm animal lover. City animal lovers can be soppy with their animals. For instance, city pet owners snuggle, have conversations, perhaps using baby-talk, and take strolls together. The pet may be kept in-doors, sleep in their owner's beds and at death get a burial with a head-stone.

Clearly that mentality is beyond the farmer's comprehension. The farmer's animals are his meal ticket. They work for him. They serve a different purpose. He cannot afford to be overly sentimental. Farmers may manage animals in groups, so each animal may not even have a name. He does relate to them in terms of the traits of the species under his care. In understanding these traits, a caring farmer can form bonds, but it's not the same as the urban pet owner.

My father, with farmer instincts, would have found highly privileged Fritz disgusting. An animal's head on a table begging? So it happened, before this visit from Bob and his family, Dad, prepared a clean, comfortable stall in a barn close by, to house the giant dog. Apparently, at the time of Bob's arrival, it was revealed to him that very comfortable quarters had been set aside for Fritz. Two successful, strong men, each used to running their own show, faced off. It was totally unacceptable to Bob to deny his dog the benefit of a house, not a barn off in the distance. He became highly insulted. Fritz would have been, as well, if he knew what was up; He, who had separation anxiety. Even though it was after dark, Bob loaded everyone back into the car and they departed to go right back to Chicago. We only saw Bob, Aunt and first cousins briefly, once after that occasion. And, again, no explanation was given to the children. In this case, my sympathy goes to all, including Fritz, but not Bob.

Speaking Southern, all I can say, is this, "Bob was just sorry white trash."

I learned from this experience to never consider taking a pet to anyone's house without an understanding beforehand If anyone comes to my home, and seems concerned about my pets, my visitor's feelings matter, even if I have to lock an animal away. To break up a family over a dog, just is a shame.

Queenie had a sister named Emily, who was an accomplished pianist, but had lapsed into schizophrenia (at an age when that condition typically falls, and there was no adequate medication at that time) and had to be hospitalized. I was told that when Queenie was visiting her sister in the hospital, she heard dreadful cursing by Emily's fellow patients. Appalled, she could not allow her precious, precocious sister stay in that environment, and determined to bring her home. To make that happen, Mr. Eddy and Queenie converted the entire upstairs into living quarters for her sister.

When we were visiting, we vaguely, understood that this upstairs was off limits to us kids. Sometimes there would come loud piano music from overhead or thumping noises. My sister, Molly, would sneak up to the head of the steps and tease Emily, which entailed a number of shoes being fired in her direction. Then Molly would dramatically race back down the stairs grinning at her own tricks. That explains some of the thumping frequently heard. It also explains a lot about Molly.

Fascinated by the mystery surrounding this chilling person above, I would creep to the head of the stairs, peak and see poor Emily squatted in a corner of the room. In the room with her, was a grand piano, and piled around her was a number of shoes ready for firing at perceived enemies like Molly. Her hair had been cut haphazardly close to her head and she had no teeth. She looked so weird. When our eyes met, she would give me a toothless grin in a friendly manner. What happened to those teeth? Did she bite people? Did grandpa pull them? Surely no one loaned her a pair of scissors to cut her own hair. We were curious and fascinated. Actually, I'm sure she was quite harmless and the matter was simply a sad one for all concerned, but then mental illness in the family was a stigma. Children, by custom, did not get unhappy family matters explained. If only we had just been told that unfortunate Emily was simply ill.

HANSEL & PEGGY IN CHICAGO

H ANSEL'S MEAD'S SISTER, Mary, was friends with our mother, Margaret Tracy. Through that association, our mother was introduced to Dad. How I'd love to know about the courtship of my father and mother. He was ten years older with a background in farming and educated as an engineer. He had been married, and divorced with three children by this first marriage. Mom always seemed to us very sedate and proper, yet there is a photo of her wearing a lowcut dress, leaning back in a chair, and dreamily staring off into space. I think most offspring would be surprised by the way we view our parents, perhaps even being shocked, by the reality of the persons they actually were as young persons.

Dad was a handsome man, very intelligent, and had a wonderful, dry sense of humor. I'm sure he was a very worldly man. We all felt he enjoyed and valued his family and we adored him. My memory holds them up as conscientious parents trying to raise proper, well-behaved children. All of us had what we call the "Mead humor," and at social gatherings, we caused laughter by telling family stories and making droll observations, just as Dad did. Considering the personalities of both of our parents, and the life we led, we had a most wonderful childhood.

⌒

My parents were living just north of Blue Island, Illinois when they had the four of us all born during the 1930s. In our immediate family, we children were each about two years apart. There was first in 1932, Hansel Byron Mead, Jr, followed by Molly Ann, myself, Marguerite Dawn and our little brother, white-haired, blue-eyed Ronald Francis. Dad had been married before Mother, so from him were step-siblings, Clifford, Charlie and Betty who were pretty well grown by the time we came along. The family doctor told Mother no more babies. Four kids two years apart and I wouldn't have had to be told.

I have mused that Byron was named after Lord Byron, the poet and Ronnie after Ronald Coleman, a well-known actor at that time. Ronnie was such a pretty baby pampered by Mother and Queenie. From pictures and memories, I would say Ronnie enjoyed and remained in that role his whole life. I have no idea how Molly and I got our names, though later after a move to Indiana, we had a cantankerous cow named Molly. That may reveal a little about Molly.

I have only Byron's memory for our time in Blue Island, Illinois, which was a part of Chicago even then. His first school was a Lutheran school in Blue Island. Before he was eight, he rode a steam engine, the Rock Island Line, then walked the rest of the way to school from the big railway yard. That seems hard to believe. He was evidently very self-reliant at a very early age.

When he was about five years old, he packed a lunch box, told his mother he was on his way to work, so she, no doubt, absorbed in other motherly concerns, bid him farewell. An alarming problem arose when, within a reasonable time he did not return from "work". After much frantic searching with the aid of tips, Grandpa learned Byron had walked down to the local train station, got on a train and had indeed gone to "work". He was discovered on a passenger car heading away down the tracks. Thank goodness for all of us and generations following, he was returned safely. He was the golden son and we all thought of him that way. As an older brother he was very protective and loving to his younger brother and sisters.

I have vivid memory of my fourth birthday. Mother arranged for me to have my birthday getting a train ride from Blue Island to Peoria. Illinois. As we were riding along, the conductor appeared beside our seat and presented me with a big, beautiful doll for a birthday present. It's a lovely memory.

In 1940, when I was going on five years old, Dad moved us to Indiana. It was the beginning of WWII. This was a significant move for Mother. It meant she would be accepting and embracing a whole new way of life during an extremely difficult time for us and the country. All their family and friends were back in the city. The area in that part of Indiana was beautiful and that surely did appeal to her. Also, from things she told me, she was rather inspired by the challenges that came her way, so different from the city life, which was her only experience. Thinking back on some of the situations and happenings we had, the manner she adapted and lived them was impressive. As life went on, until we were grown, she was introduced to many more challenges. We treasure the memories.

DOWN ON THE FARM IN A HOLLOW

O NE OF MY earliest memories involves Mother remonstrating with my father, who had our beautiful, baby brother Ronnie, about two and one-half -years- old, sitting on a log, cutting off his lovely, white curls. I was about five-years old. Dad had moved us from Chicago to a very rural community called Bean Blossom close to small town Nashville, Indiana. I think he was making a statement with that haircut. Pretty, blue-eyed boys with white curls didn't blend with that rural environment that was his childhood experience.

Mother was leaving a soft life of education, books, music, and art to a small farm at the start of the WWII. Mom and Dad would have been married about ten years at this time. A new home was in the works. but the bombing of Pearl Harbor put a halt to that. They purchased instead a log home down in a hollow in Brown County, Indiana.

Dad definitely was the lead in our family, without being authoritarian. Mother was certainly not a weak passive woman. She had strong opinions and principles. It may have been the times, but I don't remember arguments at all. In little words and gestures, he gave the impression that his Peggy was a prize. At dinner- we had to wait until she was seated before beginning to eat. If she came home from shopping, one beep of the horn and the boys were out to carry in the packages. He must have truly known and understood her character, very well. How could he have been so sure that she would be able to handle this move out of the city, down into a remote hollow on a dirt road to a log house, with no electricity? For Mother, this was more than a move, it was an absolute culture change.

The log house was typical for that place and time. We had a fireplace, wood burning kitchen stove, kerosine lamps, and an attic for us four kids; and we had a bathroom, although Dad built an outhouse to make, he said, "the place more authentic." He called it our hootenanny. He poured a slab of cement in front of it, where each of us set a foodprint, a name and date. I have also wondered, if he was setting us up in these backwoods then, as a protection, because it was the beginning of the US entering the war. He may have felt some insecurity of how it may playout, or if Chicago being an industrial city might mean danger. That hootenanny came in quite handy for children, who could go play outside and not come in for hours.

It was a small farm meant to accommodate a family of six during the war years. He bought four cows, a horse and wagon, pigs and chickens. In Dad's absence during the week, Byron and Mother would awake each morning at 5:30 a.m. to milk the cows, feed the rest of the animals and work in the garden.

Dad's farming background made him quite capable to set the farm up. He had the job in Indianapolis, Indiana about forty-five miles from the farm, and came home on the weekends. There would have to be guidance and instruction for both mother and us kids, especially nine-year-old Byron, who was to take on enormous responsibilities.

To get a garden going, Byron and Dad went out into the field to plow. Byron's instructions were to lead the horse pulling the plow down the row, while Dad walked behind the plow. But the horse stopped suddenly, and Byron looked back to see Dad lying unconscious next to the plow. Imagine the shock for Byron, a nine-year-old, who raced home to get Mother. The two of them returned to where Dad was lying, and hitched the horse up to a sled, loaded Dad onto that sled, and brought him back to the house. There would not have been an ambulance to call, and Byron doesn't remember any medical treatment other than Dad had to rest and recover. He had a bad heart and he simply over-did it. That was Dad's first heart episode, while with us.

We did have a telephone on the wall. The town had operator(s) at a switchboard and everyone had a port on the switchboard. She received a call for a certain party, then plugged into the household that received the call with their unique ring. That was called a *party-line*. I'm surprised I remember this,

but I recall our ring was two longs and a short. If someone else's ring sounded, the householder ignored it, or nosey, could quietly listen in. It wasn't wise to gossip.

We have seen so many different phones through the years; All an improvement for sure. Yet, I cannot relate to people today, so glued to their phones, answering and talking in restaurants, at the dinner table or getting panic stricken, if it is misplaced. Cell phone clutched in a hand seems to me like an obsession.

One early morning Dad answered the phone to news that a local farmer's tractor had turned over and the man was killed. Dad was very broke up about it. It was decided that we would go to the funeral being held in a small country church. We were not church goers, so Mother was unprepared for the funeral service. She was startled that the preacher conducting the service, didn't seem to be trying to offer comfort, as she expected. Instead, he seemed to be getting the congregants all worked up. Women, especially, were overcome with emotion, and running up to the casket and talking to the dead farmer. I saw a little girl from my school standing by the casket shaking all over. It was a shocking introduction to religion. When we got home, Mother announced to Dad, "No more funerals for us, Hansel. That one is enough."

∽

For four children from the city, farm animals were a never-ending joy. Children will make pets out of any animal that they can. Byron made an unlikely friendship with a chicken born with a crooked beak, so it only makes sense that she would be named, "Crooked Beak". She had a hard time eating and the other chickens bullied her unmercifully, so Byron would rescue her. When Crooked Beak was being attacked, he would pick her up and walk around with her. It got so she recognized him by sight, following him around, chirping to be picked up. When he stroked her, should she would put her head under her wing and go to sleep. He was very proud that he could have such an effect on a chicken, and the rest of us was impressed. His attentions kept her alive.

Molly and I played with dolls by the hour. She was very good at setting up little skits that we acted and conversed out various situations. She was Aunt Jane and I, Aunt Betty.

I might say, "Aunt Jane, I need to take my little, bitty baby to the doctor. She's feverish."

Aunt Jane might say, "Oh, heaven's, Aunt Betty. I'll just stay right here and take care of all our children. You just run right along."

One of my dolls was a large, rag doll my mother made for me. I dearly loved that doll. I named her Belinda. I hauled her everywhere and slept with her. I think she was the equivalent to a child's favorite *blankie*. If you've had a child attached to a blanket, you know that even if you have to back-track twenty miles for a forgotten blanket, it has to be done. Once, I washed a *blankie* belonging to my son, Kevin, and hung it on the line. He was a hyperactive boy and when it became too quiet, too long, I needed to check. I ran to the window and checked the yard. There stood my little four-year-old under the clothes line, the blankie in his fist held up against his cheek, yet still attached to the clothes line. He was seldom so still, so I didn't interrupt

My Belinda evidently became quite dirty so, Mother took her apart to wash her. Seeing my distress, Mother assured me that she would sew Belinda back together, only she never did. To this day, I hug a pillow to sleep, and the joke has been made that the pillow is my *Belinda*. It's no wonder I've had to have psychiatric care, deprived as I was of my Belinda.

Dad made a doll house for Molly and me, that was very detailed. There was a stairway in it that had a handrail made with matchsticks. Sometimes Mother would throw a large blanket over a table, so we could crawl under and play, Aunt Jane and Aunt Betty.

Mother must have taught herself to can vegetables, make jelly and pickle. It was a necessity, but it also meant we had fresh vegetables, hard to come by in the city. I remember she stuffed bell peppers with cabbage soaked in a large crock pot and fermented like sauerkraut. We loved them. And one favorite Indiana farm dish introduced to us by our father was Corn Bread Gravy, made with left-over cornbread from last night's supper. Fresh would do. We still love it to this day.

Cornbread Gravy

Left-over corn bread
Chopped bacon
Scrambled Eggs (1 egg per person)
White cream sauce (2 cups for two servings)

Fry the bacon until crisp. To the leavings,
pour in the eggs and scramble.
When done, add the white sauce in with
the scrambled eggs and bacon crisps
Ladle up a hefty amount of the egg gravy
over a slice of cornbread and enjoy
*(*To us Meads, this beats southern
White Gravy and Biscuits)

We had four milking cows that, when fresh, provided us with fresh milk, skimmed cream. churned butter and butter milk. Never has cold butter milk tasted as good as that did. How impressive that Mother had to learn all this in short order and did.

In the winter, Dad awakened us, by wiggling our toes and chanting poems like:

A Dairy cow is a thing of charm
It lifts its tail and fills the barn

Or from an Indiana poet, James Whitcome Riley,

When the frost is on the punkin and the fodder's   .
in the shock,

I was sleep-walking one night and tumbled down the steps from the attic. Dad rescued me and sat with me on his lap until I stopped crying. That was worth the fall. I spent a lot of time on Daddy's lap. Molly, too, walked in her sleep. Once Dad brought home a bushel basket of apples, and Molly walking in her sleep sat down on the bushel of apples and peed. After that, he would hold up a rusty pair of pliers he had, and state that Molly's pee had caused that.

Mother saw to it that we had books. In the evening when home, Dad would read to us. I loved books and stories and still do. I recollect, he in an easy chair in front of the fire in the fireplace, with his pipe, its smell and we kids gathered on the floor at his feet. Being all together in that warm room being read to was such a cozy, secure pleasure. One book that stands out was Tom Sawyer. He would read it by chapter night after night. Well, the night he read the chapter that had Tom and Becky lost in the cave, I was completely caught up with the terror of their situation. He finished the chapter, stopped, emptied his pipe, and said quietly, "Time for bed."

"What?", I cried. "He's still in that cave with Becky!" He very, firmly put us to bed. Youngsters did not disobey then or argue, though I tended to. Certainly, we didn't want to displease our daddy. We went to bed, but all wrought up over Tom and Becky's situation.

There was a knot hole in the attic floor, that allowed us to lie on our bellies, and peak down into the living room and see Dad and Mom reading in front of the fire. One night one of us spied mom smoking a cigarette. That was big news. For some time we would take turns to verify the authenticity of this sighting. There is no memory of her smoking at any other time before or since, so she must have been doing so to be companiable with dad and his pipe.

Close to the house was a clear creek. Mother had the distinct belief that if a person could turn themselves over on their back to float, he/she would not drown. So, we each mastered that skill quickly, because with that we could go swimming without supervision. I try to remember, but I do not recall if we wore bathing suits. I do know in the summer that we were bathed once a week in a wash tub in the yard waiting our turn in the nude. Certainly we need not worry with visitors.

We were truly isolated, though further down the dirt road, there was an older brother and sister farming couple. They owned two gentle mules, and the farmer would put us on their backs and lead us around. Way on down beyond them, was a family we called Lukass with twenty children. We had only occasional contact with those children. I don't know why. They had to pass our house to go to school, when they went to school. One morning one of the girls needed to use the toilet, so Mother directed her to our bathroom. She had to show her about the flusher on the toilet. At school, she exclaimed about our toilet, "You could just push a little handle and all the stink goes down." Once after a heavy rain storm, their Model T came floating down the creek and past our house.

My mother hated guns, and Byron wanted a BB gun. I'm sure daddy was for it, but Mother was not. He got it, but he was not to shoot at or near any person, and if he broke the rule, she'd wrap the thing around a tree. One winter day with oxfords and two pairs of socks he put the end of the barrel on the toe of his shoe and shot a BB. It didn't hurt, so Molly, wanted him to shoot the BB gun at her shoe. Well, he did. Then, yowling, she ran to Mother and told on him. It was typical Molly, teasing, again and he was in trouble, which was rare.

I don't know if before or after, but that was one of two dramatic happenings with the gun. The other incident involved a pig. The breed of pigs Dad chose for us were huge. Pigs have large litters and frequently there is one born that is a runt. The mother hog will either kill the runt or the other little piggies will not share a teat, so the runt dies. Mother could not let that happen. Dad had let her know a nursing mama pig can be very dangerous. When there came a litter with a runt, Mother decided to sneak in the pen while the mother pig was nursing. Her plan was to grab the runt and climb out. So, she did. She counted on the mother being so absorbed in the bliss of feeding the piglets, she wouldn't notice the intruder. Wrong! Byron put himself on guard duty with his BB gun. For some reason even he can't explain, he fired a BB at the mama pig. Ping! Mama pig apparently had an eye out as well, and spied Mother. At once, she was up, squealing, grunting, piggies dropping from her teats, and went for Mother. Byron, shocked, saw Mother running for the fence and as he tells it with awe in his voice. "She took that fence backwards!" She managed to keep the baby in her arms and brought it into the house. We had a wood burning kitchen stove, so she opened the oven door fixed a little nest there to keep it warm and alive, however at some point, the oven door flew shut and threw the piggy in the oven. It's amazing how loud and all the different noises a pig has at its disposal to communicate. Fortunately, this pig's noise of alarm was ear-splitting, and baby pig lived to be a pet. I don't remember how long we petted him, but eventually I'm sure we had him for dinner.

THE LITTLE RED ONE-ROOM SCHOOL HOUSE

IN THE WINTER Byron woke up in the cold attic, to do home chores then walked to the school to bring in wood and draw a bucket of water. The one stove in the school would be going full blast to keep the room warm in the winter. And the bucket of water? Each pupil had a cup with our name on it and drank from the bucket of water when thirsty. To this day I have a wonderful immunity to colds or flu. I'm sure I got it in Brown County from dipping our cups in that community bucket of water.

The school we were to attend was a walk about a mile up our dirt road, to a paved two-lane road where sat the red school house on a hill. It was one room for eight eight grades. In the center of the room, was that stove Byron collected wood for. Outside was an outhouse. I hated going outside to that dark outhouse. It had curse words written on the walls and our mother did not approve of cuss word (though I can't imagine how I knew what was a cuss word) so I felt wicked just reading those words. Of course, I had to check if they were still there each time I was in there. We walked to school and it *was* up hill and it was through all kinds of weather. In our case a true hardship.

On a very cold, day, Byron as usual rose at 5:30 a.m. to

feed the pigs and chickens, milk the cows, then to school to get in the wood, and bucket of water. A farm widow in the corner house across from the school, stopped him to ask, "Son, whatever are you doing out here this cold morning?"

He replied, "I'm getting the wood and water for school".

She said, "Oh, son, don't you know that its twenty below this morning and the school is closed!"

At first Mama sent Byron to school in Chicago knickerbockers. You can't imagine. They were baggy pants, probably corduroys, that came to the knees with knee high socks and ankle high shoes. Oh, he was a dandy. His school mates, wearing faded, ill-fitting overalls, carrying lard buckets for lunch, must have been astonished, as if he were a foreigner invading their midst. I remember coming to the door of the school house, and there was my dear brother in combat with a horde of males in overalls. out-numbered by far. It was because of those knickerbockers! Dad should have warned her. Byron likes to tell it that I flew down the steps and launched into the battle with fists flying, even climbing the boys' backs. I did manage to bloody one boy's nose, which ended the battle. I'm sure I was wearing a dress. No slacks or shorts in that day, you can be sure. After that, knickerbockers for Byron were abandoned for overalls.

He and I must have bonded with that incident, and have remained so.

At school, we stood in the front of the room for spelling bees. reading and multiplication tables. There was singing. It was customary for the Superintendent of Schools came to these country schools probably for inspection purposes. I remember ours was a Story Teller. These old story tellers, didn't read stories, the told stories with much enthusiasm and skill. Where we were, our superintendent, took the time to do some first class story-telling, standing in front of the room. If you have not heard a folksy story teller, you've missed out. Story telling can be quite a talent. He kept us enthralled with stories, including some long and scary.

Because there was a war on, there was a shortage of paper. How did the teacher compensate? We each had to bring a roll of toilet paper to school and on that we did many ovals, practiced our ABCs and cursive. When that memory came to mind, I became curious concerning the paper selection, so I decided to Google, *toilet paper in the 1940's*. The first site that popped up was titled, "Splinter-free toilet paper didn't exist until the 1930's." That certainly caught my attention. There are numerous sites that reveal headlines regarding the shortage of toilet paper, during WWII, so that would be the explanation. Tablets and school paper was hard to come by. I even learned toilet paper was doled out in a soldiers' rationing pack. When Covid first struck, I saw news reports of people stripping the stores of toilet paper, which I found puzzling. Now I think it was my generation of folks, remembering their old WWII days and a shortage of toilet paper.

I think there was only about twenty-five of us in all eight grades. I remember a big, hulking farm boy in a row next to mine, who sort of scared me. There was a lot to be admired of those teachers in that one room with eight grades Later when I was in the fourth grade, we went to a regular school with one grade in each room and we had no trouble at all with the transition and all made the honor roll. My saved reports cards, showed A's and B's, but C in self- control. Dad would carefully review our report cards and dole out rewards for A's. Through the years, there were continued problems with self-control on my part.

When pretty, boy, Ronnie, was in first grade, he sat on the teachers lap and combed her hair. I thought that was outrageous and told Mama so. "Just ask him, "I demanded of her, "I bet he can't even say his ABC's!" It may very well have been the teacher's fault. That continued to be a pattern with Ronnie and women. Molly got the same attention from boys.

That stove, that Byron carried wood to was just sitting in the center of with no protective barrier around it. While I was returning to my desk after leaving the teacher, I tripped over a piece of wood near the red hot stove and mashed my hand onto the side of that it. Byron walked me home howling in pain, constantly putting cold snow on my hand and trying his best to comfort me. Mother rose to the occasion with the accepted cure of the day by smearing butter on my searing hand, but the snow was probably the best that could have been done.

After we had outgrown our city clothes, Mother would have had to make dresses for Molly's and me. Farm food and flour came in large bags that were covered in flowered cotton, so the sacks were preserved with care. We would eye those bags before they were empty deciding on ownership. Molly and I wore feed sack dresses at home and to school. A war was on, after all. Everything was rationed. Also, there were rag and clothes-pin dolls, Mama made. Brand new lace-up, oxford shoes were bought at the beginning of the school year. By spring, but before school was out, our toes would have reached the toe end. A simple solution was to cut out the front end of the shoe to relieve the pressure. I try to imagine my kids going to school with the toes cut out of their shoes. They would have been embarrassed, and rightly so. Then, there was no embarrassment in that for us, because the other kids were wearing the same style shoe.

ACCIDENTS AND AILING

B ECAUSE OF THE war and location, medical doctors were not readily available. At that time, one went to the doctor, if very sick or badly injured, not for checkups. Dad did all the doctoring on the animals and us. I enjoyed overturning large rocks to check for any varmints found there. One day after a check, I dropped a large, heavy rock back down on my big toe. It didn't hurt at first, but when I got on a swing, looked down and saw my toe was a dirty bloody mess, then I howled. Thank goodness Dad was home, and they determined I'd need some repair and stitches. Perhaps Mother couldn't face what was to be done or had to stay with the other kids, it was Dad who drove me to a doctor about fifteen miles away. There wasn't anything for pain, or anything antiseptic, so Dad had to hold me down while the doc put my mangled toe together with stitches. It was terrifying and painful for both myself and Dad. I also managed to step on a board and run two rusty nails into the bottom of my foot. Again, Dad held me down, while the doctor cleaned up the openings because of the fear of lock jaw. Iodine glycerin was Dad's medicinal treatment, of choice. He had it made up by a pharmacist. He swabbed our sore throats with it, and put it on cuts. It was not just a traditional medicine, because it did help with infections of any kind.

We did catch all the childhood diseases, because babies and children were not vaccinated against them. Later all of us except Dad, got scarlet fever, which was a very serious, infectious disease. That disease brought a visiting nurse to our house and got a very large sign on the door with the word **QUARANTINED** in big, red letters. Dad plodded up and down the attic steps every few hours dabbing our throats with the concoction he firmly believed in, iodine glycerin. We all pulled through without any serious, medical problems, though Ronnie was deaf for a small time and ended up a stutterer. There was a small article in the Nashville paper that stated the Dawn Mead had scarlet fever. No HIPPA then, that's for sure.

We had a crab apple tree at the farm. I sat up in that, once, and devoured the wonderful sour apples until quite full. The consequences of that required a doctor's consultation, because the stomach ache I acquired soon after certainly got everyone's attention. It was alarming, noisy but thorough.

Other than that, I remember only one more accident potentially very serious. There had been a bad storm and Dad was due home from work, so Byron and Mother decided that the road to the house needed some fixing in order for Dad to able to make the drive home. Byron hitched the horse to the large spring wagon so that he and Molly went up the road to dig for rocks and gravel to do repairs on potholes. After getting a load, Molly clambered up on the wagon and startled the horse. Off it took. Byron had chased the wagon down, scrambled aboard, and lunged for the reins wanting to stop the horse, but didn't succeed. That horse was heading home top speed. Galloping pell-mell around a corner the wagon tipped over. Out flew Byron through a briar patch and onto the dry creek bed. He did get a broken shoulder.

There was a local woman who was in a mental crisis. Mental illness had such a stigma, that usually the suffering person was kept at home whenever possible and protected. If the person was a woman, and her age was right, family and women friends could blame a woman's bazaar behavior on menopause. Even with that explanation, the word menopause was said in a lowered voice with nodding of heads and murmurs of sympathy. Men, including doctors, tended to view emotional problems to women having a hysteric nature. Sadly, this lady's condition deteriorated from bad to worse; it reached such a state, she needed to be removed from her home. When it came to Mother's attention, the woman had been put in the local jail for safe keeping. Mother was aghast, so she sought to befriend her. She had Dad deliver items that might be a comfort and support for the lady in a jail. Dad would have risen to the occasion to turn on the charm. That backfired. Some time went by and one early morning while Mom and Dad were still in bed, they were awakened by the sheriff and the demented lady in their house and at their bedside. With her hands on her hips the woman, angrily demanded, "And what is the meaning of this, may I ask?" In her troubled state, the visits from a handsome man, stirred up a romantic notion, that she had a lover bringing her the nice, little gifts. When released from jail or while confined, she convinced the sheriff to hunt the lover down. Mother loved that story. I wish we had the letter she wrote home about that experience.

The years we spent on the farm were war years. Life for everyone in the Western world was involved with hardship, sacrifice and loss. Father worked as an engineer to provide for his family, and I search my memory, knowing there was deprivation, yet we did not feel deprived. Dad had set us up for success, and that lessened much hardship for us. We had it so much better than most. How grateful he must have ben to have had such a complement in a wife. Mother deserves such admiration, that she with four children, nine years and under, accepted a whole new way of life and lived it so well.

BROWN COUNTY STATE PARK (BCSP)

AS A POLITICAL favor, our father was offered the job as superintendent of Brown County State Park, in Central Indiana. He was a natural for this kind of work. He had spent some of his childhood in Brown County. He was a hard worker. creative and had a bona fide public relations personality, enhanced by his keen sense of humor. It is a park of about of 16,000 acres in central Indiana just south of Indianapolis. That part of Indiana is made up of rolling hills, very scenic, so that it has always attracted artists. That charmed my artistic mother, who was very pleased to be living there in that lovely countryside. She painted little after arriving there, no doubt, because she was involved with helping my father. Park-work, during peak seasons, is very demanding with no set hours. In addition to helping Dad, she had the primary care of four children. To me as a child, the town of Nashville is where we went to school, and -did our shopping. Now it is an interesting, picturesque village, that is an artist colony. It is fun to walk through, with shops of art, crafts and good eating establishments.

The park had two lakes, a big lodge with cottages, a riding stable with a rodeo arena, and huge swimming pool. We were free to go wherever we wished. Our house and yard were surrounded by a log fence. There was a big service building, that was just across the yard from our house with a large concrete space. That building also housed Dad's office. We were able to wander out where the caged animals and picnic areas were. The park was so spread out, that we often caught a ride with Dad to see other parts of the park. There were plenty of fascinating areas to visit when entertaining ourselves.

A few years ago I coordinated a group of seniors on a trip to Nashville and the park. I'm elderly now, and it was exciting to me to experience the beauty of the park and sense the familiarity. We stayed at the Abe Martin Lodge, that was very comfortable and rustic. I remembered that Abe Martin was a cartoon character, a cranky, hillbilly, that appeared in the Indianapolis newspaper in the 1930s. The author became a resident in Brown County about the same time the large acreage was set aside to be a state park. A rustic lodge was built in the park, and it appropriately received the name, Abe

M DAWN DAYTON

Martin Lodge. The Lodge had a restaurant where my sister, Molly waited tables.

The scrapbook Mother kept from that time has many letters of commendation written to both dad, Mother and the Indiana Park Service from individuals and groups, complimentary to the accommodating welcome they received while at the park. We were then four children from six to fourteen years. People paid to visit this wonderful place and it was our back yard.

SCHOOL WHILE LIVING AT THE PARK

W HEN WE FIRST moved into the park, Molly, Ronnie and myself, attended the school in the small-town Nashville not far outside the gates of the park. Bryon had started high school that year and Mother drove him to Bloomington, Indiana. Nashville was a tiny town with one school that only went up only to the eighth grade. There each grade had its own room; we did fine. The one-room school house with one teacher had us right where we were supposed to be. The school had a big metal tube off one side of the building as an escape route for the second floor in case of fire.

This was the time of the world-wide polio scare. Mother was obviously worried. The media had accounts of crippled children and people in iron lungs. Because of its availability, we spent a lot of time at the pool, which increased our risk for catching it. Then there was a vaccine and it came to our school. The vaccine was given in the school office and a long line snaked out down the hall. The school was abuzz, that the shot was given by an army nurse with a gigantic needle. While standing in line, hearing this and seeing children walking away in tears, I became positively hysterical. The school had to call Mother. When she arrived, there was her fourth grade daughter still in line. At the sight of Mother, I leaped astraddle of her begging to go home. Instead, I got the vaccine, but I had my mother for comfort.

In the fourth grade I had an awfully mean teacher named Miss Stalker. I have a clear memory of her as a tall, thin woman with white hair, pulled severely back from her face. One day she was standing over a frightened girl, harshly berating her. The girl was not guilty of the offence she was being accused of. My sense of justice and my lack of self-control prevailed. I impulsively protested, which was bad enough, but I did so without raising my hand. Quietly, that horrid teacher said to me, "Young lady, come with me to the cloak room." There was a small, narrow room off each classroom for our coats, goulashes and lunches. Once In the cloakroom, not saying a word, she turned me towards her, and slapped me hard across my face. So keen is my memory of this, that I remember the loose flesh on her face tremble from her slap. I was consumed with shame and fear. I didn't tell my parents or anyone.

Later, the janitor caught me at lunchtime jumping desks and paddled me, not hard or angry. He was a fatherly figure and didn't even seem cross. I don't remember being upset. Daddy did take offence at that. Because of that incident, Mother somehow got us accepted in the Indiana State University demonstration school in Bloomington, Indiana about twenty miles away. I remember being tested, but didn't understand what it was for. The first year she drove us. Soon other kids, as well as us were bussed from Brown County to Bloomington. We had to be driven out to the entrance of the park to meet the bus. Later Byron, at age sixteen, got his driver's license and did the driving.

Children at that school, were a more urban society of children. A girl in my fifth-grade class at that school had a slumber party and I was invited. I certainly had never spent the night away from home or with other kids. Apparently, I got really hyper and was acting out. I was mortified, because I realized that the mother obviously wanted me gone. Dad and Mother were about twenty miles away, and I would never have asked to go home or known to call, so I could get home. I was just achingly miserable until I did get there. It was just one more incidence that my hyper personality got me in trouble and I was so ashamed.

I think I was a bundle of contradictions. I was non-stop running, climbing and wrestling, but also had baby dolls and played happily with them. As active as I was, I loved to read and to Mother's relief I could sit in a chair to read for hours. I wonder if there is anyone still alive that remember the story book series, "The Bobbsey Twins". I just loved them and that let to other books.

WHERE DO TO PLAY IN THE PARK?

W E HAD A beautiful scenic view from our house. All in our immediate area that was available by walking or bicycle There were woods with a deep ravine near our house. We found a grape vine on the edge of the ravine. We learned that with a hard run and firm grip, it would launch us up and over the ravine, a distance of about twelve feet across. We managed to keep a grip, because none of us landed in the ravine. Dangerous, yes, but we kids had so much freedom to roam, explore and play. Hours went by when we would be on bikes, or hanging out where the public was.

My bike was a used boy's bike, with a new seat cover and a home-paint job. I leaped on that bike to go in any direction for any little reason. When thirsty or hungry, I went home dumped the bike on its side, went in to attend to my needs, back out, jumped on the bike and was off in another direction. I rode without holding the handlebars and tried doing tricks every chance I got.

I have always loved to ride a bike, so when I retired from work a few years ago, I put an ad on Craig's list: *"Two old fogies recently retired, looking to ride bikes. Want to buy 2 bikes'"* We got just what we advertised for from one source.

To our pleasure, they were barely used then and haven't been for some time since—They're gathering dust in the garage. There's good reason for that.

The Ad was answered by a seller who had them in storage after buying them for his in-laws, that had been unable to use them. They were older models, but not as old as we were.

How pleased we were, buying two matching 10-speed bikes, far more modern than I had ever ridden with those attachments for gears and brakes on handle bars. I couldn't wait, just couldn't wait, until I got ours home to show my stuff to my husband, Bill. Surely age would be no handicap. We took our first ride that day. I shoved off with a great deal of confidence, then suddenly the front wheel seemed to wobble. The dog knew to get out of the way, but the car did not. I side swiped my little Corolla making a 10-inch scrape down the front fender, jerked the handle bars the other way and fell down, fortunately in the grass next to the driveway. Bill charged out of garage shaking his head. "Good grief, Dawn, can't you be more careful?" He obviously had not taken a careful appraisal of the situation, because the mishap was not due to my carelessness. I pointedly made a check of the front wheel; it was not loose. I just needed to get used to the bike. Of course, I failed to factor in that nearly sixty years has gone by since I was top of my game, so to speak.

The next day Bill and I ventured out for our first companionable spin on our bikes. He proceeded down the drive ahead of me to the center of our cul-de-sac. I impressively cleared the Corolla heading full tilt toward him; did a quick check on my gears. Why? I didn't even know how they work! Simultaneously he stopped, to looks back to be sure I was on my way. Whoops! I crashed into him and the bike.. Down we went— Right in the middle of the cul-de-sac. We fell his way, so he hit the concrete hard with me on top. My shoes flew through the air. A real pileup. Before we untangled ourselves from the wreckage, we were both frantically checking out our new neighborhood to see if we were being observed. We think we weren't. Can you get a visual of two elderly people in a heap tangled with a bike and each other? Now this really made old Bill cross, "Dawn, for heaven's sake watch where you're going," as if it were entirely my fault. *He* stopped dead in my path to reassure himself I was coming. Well, I was. I just forgot the brake was by my hand and not under my feet, as they were on the bikes of old.

Then one day my dear little granddaughter, Annie, was visiting along with her tricycle. While I was leisurely riding in the cul-de-sac, she suddenly darted toward me on her tricycle. I whipped the front wheel away and crashed into the mailbox. Good thing we have a trellis on it. I managed to grab that before going down into the flowers and ripped it loose. Apparently, the fall was a was a dramatic one, because my neighbor hollered, "Are you alright, Dawn?" She later told me that when we are out riding, she and her husband rush to the window to watch.

I didn't know what to make of that. Was it concern or seeking a little entertainment? So the bikes reminded me that I was indeed growing old and they now gather dust in the garage.

Growing old is a very gradual process, full of unpleasant surprises. Little things are taken away piece by piece. I, who never wins a prize, nor have been elected president or queen, am now the *oldest* wherever I go—That's something.

Years ago, I was commiserating with a very, elderly lady about aging. I complained that I had to wake up each morning, wondering what new ache or pain would greet me. She agreed, and said, "When I first wake up, I don't open my eyes. I just flap my arms in and out sideways and, if they don't hit the wooden sides of something, I figure I'm still alive and I say to myself, *'Lady, get up and get moving'*

↜

Dad made us stilts from lightweight wood poles with wedges for feet about twelve inches from the ground. It was a little tricky to get upright and begin to walk. They served for self-entertainment or competition. Sometime we kids made our own from tree limbs; They were awfully hard on shoes. I don't think a child today would even know what they were.

Close by our house was that service building that had a large concrete floor for servicing park equipment, a work shop, Dad had installed a drink and snack machines on that large service floor, along with a juke box. So, when the building emptied out in the evening, we would use it as a skating rink with the juke box blaring. Oh, the joy of it. I would skate and sing. I especially loved singing, "Lavender Blue Dilly, Dilly. Lavender Green" popular at that time at the top of my lungs for hours on end it seemed. I loved when Molly skated and sungwith me, she performing skating twirls and skating backwards.

One evening while all of us kids were in the service building, Ronnie was pushing me on the mechanic's creeper. I was kneeling on it as Ronnie was pushing me head-long across that concrete floor. I was loving it, until the wheels locked. I pitched forward smacking my face on the concrete, and chipped my two front teeth. I picked up those chips; walked home and presented them to Mother. Mom looked at Dad and sadly said, "Oh, Hansel, look what she's done now"

I didn't understand the enormity of it at that time, but I was left with what I consider fangs, along with an inherited gap between my two front teeth. My parents never got them capped. Orthodontist weren't a given then and, unfortunately, not every face with an overbite or misshapen teeth got braces or caps. Later in my forties I tried getting braces to eliminate the gap. The day I got the braces off, my younger son, Greyson, about age eight, came out to greet me. As he hugged me, he stared into my face, and warmly said. "Oh, mom...you look.

you look, well not pretty, but a lot better." So much for never a nice grin for eighty two years. I would remind myself to just smile, not grin. Sad thing is I love to laugh, head flung back, boisterous, uncontrollable. With that floor accident in mind, you can visualize me as a hyperactive, chipped tooth, fang face, laughing.

⌒

At that time and place, square dancing was big. Women would dress up in twirly skirts, men in overalls and brogans. The locals provided music with fiddles, guitars, pianos, whatever and whoever had the instruments and talent participated. A square dance is a dance for four couples, or eight dancers in total, arranged in a square, with one couple on each corner, facing the middle of the square. The dancers are prompted or cued through a sequence of steps by a <u>caller,</u> who calls them out as the music plays, sometime dancing himself, or standing nearby.

When I think back on this, I can feel the music and hear the calls in my head. I would never have become a ballerina and to this day am self-conscious about dancing, but I threw myself heart and soul into square dancing.

⌒

Living in the park, our associates were the public and school. We weren't in on the fads, crazes and demands of a certain generation. As a result we were still very naïve regarding racial matters, not even noticing that our world had no black/brown people in it. What we never knew or thought about, Indiana was a segregated state with a history of racial discrimination and definitely violence related to racial issues. When we were there, Civil rights were a long way off. We weren't guilty of racism; It just didn't exist for us. So much of what has been my experience and formed my feelings, came to me in bits and pieces. It first hit me in the beautiful Brown County State Park.

When I was an adult Mother told me what to her was a sweet story. In Chicago where there was rampant racism and racial slurs were accepted and common, she was determined we kids would not be racially biased. She carefully schooled us that the black people called negroes (she over did this with an exaggerated "Nee'groes) and were lovely people. She probably was as naïve as we were. The story was, that when I was four years old, she took me down-town Chicago to Marshall Fields, and as we stepped into an elevator, there stood a black, overweight lady. Mother's buildup must have stuck, because to Mother's astonishment, I walked straight over to that lady. flung my arms around her and said, "Hello, you, nice, fat nee'gro, you." To Mother's relief, the lady was intelligent, absorbed my age and obvious sincerity, and responded in kind, enfolding me in a big hug right back.

Mother read to us from the Uncle Remus stories, so I

insisted, when I grew up, my babies were going to be just like those pictured, because they were so "cute." When I would voice this to Mother, she'd say vaguely, "We'll see, Dawnie. We'll just have to wait and see."

A word on Uncle Remus. If one is familiar with these stories through books and Disney, you might have the impression, that the author is making light of black children, but that is not the case. Joel Chandler Harris, the author, born shortly before the Civil War, was an illegitimate child, with not a lot of security as a child. At age fourteen, he quit school to work, and was farmed out to a plantation in Georgia. I read in one biography that while there and lonely, he would go down to the barn, where there was an elderly black man who gathered the children together in the barn and told them stories. That experience stayed with young Joel, so that later, he became a well-known American journalist and folklorist; Thus we have Uncle Remus and his delightful series of stories. Later Disney, picked up on these, and American got the "Songs of the South." I believe, considering the man, who wrote, these stories brought honor to an old black man on a plantation, whose story telling brought some light in to the dark lives of these black children and for generations of children for years to come.

The pool was the scene of an event that had a major impact on my life-long racial views. One day I was coming out of the pool into the entrance area with the dressing rooms and long counter for paying customers. Behind the counter was my father among other men, all stone faced; in front of the counter was a group of Cub Scouts, my age, in uniform milling around. It was crowded, but quiet. I could sense something *off*; I distinctly remember feeling uneasy. Mother startled me by grabbing my hand, and sternly saying, "Come on, Dawnie, were going home!" and rushed me out to the park's truck, which was facing the fence. Inside the truck, she immediately, threw her head down on the steering wheel, pointing toward the fence and began to cry. That was high drama for Mother. There, a few feet away, was a little boy about my age, in his Cub Scout uniform. He had crept behind the bushes, was kneeling, hands holding the fence with face pressed into it, watching his fellow scouts swimming.

He was black! He couldn't go into the pool. It was the law and worse yet, the custom. I must have sensed the conflict taking place at that entrance. I'm sure my mother would have contended. I hope my dad would have. What an enormous, but silent, load of disagreement it was. I think back— why couldn't the leader simply refuse the swim for the entire troupe? It would have been a great teaching event. That is today's thinking or action. Should he pull all the boys in a spirit of fair play, or deny the one? I want to think of him as a decent fellow. After all he had that little boy in the troupe and it was in the 1940s. What would that decision entail? By denying all the boys, he would have to deal with hostility among the parents of disappointed boys, all because of a little black boy. By denying the one, he would not to have any conflict except within himself. I still ache when I picture that little fellow in the blue scout uniform looking through that fence to the tune of my strong mother crying. Why didn't we stay, or treat him to an ice cream, and tell him how handsome he was in his blue scout uniform? We just left him there. Whatever did he tell his parents or did he? The painful scaring on that boy scaring from that experience would have had far-reaching effects The impact on him would have been far worse on him than on me—all my life it has haunted me.

I continued to love that pool. I swam for hours and when I went home, I'd see rings around lights from being under chlorine water so long. One summer my hair turned green from the chlorine. I remember two female lifeguards trying to wash it out.

There was a drowning once. I was standing right close by, when I saw a man, wading to the edge of the pool carrying a limp body of a small boy. The boy just looked dead! I was shocked. The pool was very crowded. The man was the father of the boy, who also happened to be a physician. I watched as he was doing artificial respiration trying to resuscitate his son, then use his stethoscope, then flung it down in frustration. All the while he was crying loudly. I started running and I just kept on running around and around the pool. I had to be chased down and stopped. I was feeling the adult man's anguish and was simply overwhelmed. Dad told us later the boy had a bad heart defect, and the father had taken his eyes momentarily away from the child to look up to see him floating. Being the father and a physician, he couldn't help but blame himself for the death.

From pictures now at the park, I see the big old pool has had to be replaced. In my memory it was huge. The shallow end was a large oval area and then a rectangular deep end, room for a high dive and low diving board. It was surrounded by a high chain link fence with bushes alongside it. We could spend all day at that pool. There was always a vehicle to catch a ride down there and get a ride home. We lived in the higher elevation within the park, so when older, I'd ride my bike down a long sloping road, to the pool and at closing someone would bring me and the bike home.

We kids were all good swimmers. With our next move that was to Florida, we lived on a lake and had to be lifeguards, among our many other duties. The creek and pool prepared us well.

It took so little to entertain us. We all read. And the radio could be thrilling. I still remember the music used to introduce Inner Sanctum, a scary mystery. There was Gene Autry, the singing cowboy singing "I'm back in the Saddle Again." A Detroit, Michigan station broadcasted the radio show, The Lone Ranger, using the William Tell Overture as the theme song. And there was eerie, eerie Invisible Man."

Between the narrator, the music and above all the sound effects, those broadcasters could create mental visuals and emotional responses that were so authentic, we would be spellbound. Try going on-line and pull up Inner Sanctum an old radio show. Listen to the narration and sound effects.

We also attended movies in someone's barn with a sheet tacked up for a screen. We thought Abbot and Costello were hysterically funny. We were thrilled with the movie set-up, clustered with other children on hay in a barn. It was the mid-1950s before we got a black and white TV with its snowy screen, but it did not bring the excitement that we experienced grouped together in fear or laughter before a radio.

⌒

It's surprising that I didn't become more involved at the riding stables. I loved horses and day-dreamed about riding. That was the time of Gene Autry and Tonto, and Roy and Dale Evens the singing cowboys. They rode and sang and did away with all the bad guys. Dad would take us to the drive-in with Ronnie and I armed with cap pistols. As we watched those old westerns, during the shooting scenes, Ronnie and I hung out the windows and would shoot away at the bad guys.

I so admired Dale Evans. She wore a cowboy hat, cowboy boots and would run at her horse and swiftly leap astride. Byron wore cowboy boots and when he outgrew them, I took them over. They were way too large but I wore them until my feet were blistered. I so longed for a horse to jump on and gallop away.

The riding stables held a rodeo one year. Mother took us to see it. Rodeos really are exciting. One skill in the arena was a horseman who would chase down a calf, rope it, leap off the horse and tie up the calf. That was the competition. Who could accomplish that the fastest won a prize. While seated in the stands taking in this event, with no explanation, Mother stood up and firmly announced, "That's it. I've had enough. We're going home."

We protested, "It's not over, Mama. We want to stay and watch it some more."

"No more," she declared, "We're leaving." And we did. On the way home she revealed to us that she was upset about the calves. After the calf was tied up, the riders had to clear the field for the next competitor, so with the rope still around the calf the cowboy simply rode off the field dragging the calf behind them. Mother was sickened by the cruelty. There were no further rodeos for us.

It happened at that same rodeo, there was a raffle in the works for two beautiful Arabian white mares, named Tillie and Tessie, and each had a colt. Along with all that were saddles, bridles and a surrey. Byron won the raffle. It seems rather suspect to me now, that the park superintendent's fifteen-year-old son won the raffle, but I prefer to think that was a coincidence. What is more likely, it could be he stacked the deck by buying hundreds of tickets. The two mares were so pretty. Shortly after that he was hitching the two mares to a surrey and providing customers surrey rides around the park for the price of twenty five cents a head. At some time thereafter, Tessie developed a leg tumor, and had to be put down, but Tillie remained with us for a while.

Once I went down to the barn, and snuck Tillie out, got a bridle on her, climbed aboard her bareback and coaxed her for a walk down the road. She must have taken it in her head that I was a no Dale Evans, because she suddenly spun around and headed back to the barn at a gallop. I was holding on to her mane and squeezing my knees for dear life. I had opened the barn door just wide enough to sneak her out. As she galloped toward the barn door, I had to pull my knees up for fear of being scraped off. She shot through a narrow doorway and into her stall. It scared me silly. I had taken her out without permission, so I don't think I ever told anybody about that incident either.

We also had a couple of cows at that barn that Byron milked. I was usually following him while he milked. Once I was trying to ride the calf as he was milking. Byron was very annoyed with me because the mama cow was nervous about the calf and wouldn't let down her milk. I did manage to get on the calf, which promptly took off jumping wildly, dumping me in a ditch. It knocked the breath out of me. I was hurt physically but, more so, that my beloved Byron continued to bawl me out and showed me no sympathy, even though I was gasping for breath.

I don't know if Dad ever boxed or just liked boxing, but he kept a pair of 16-ounce boxing gloves he would occasionally put on me to show me how to box. I took great pride in my ability to wrestle, as well, even though I was a skinny runt. Dad had an employee, who had a son my age. Once Dad got this boy and I along with the boy's father in an empty room in the service building for us to box with those huge boxing gloves. Anything to please my dad, I fought my heart out. I don't remember the outcome. It really didn't matter. What I do remember is Mama learned about the fight and was angry. It was not about the boxing itself. She was angry because Dad was betting on me to be the winner, his little daughter, for heaven's sake. He defended himself saying, "Peggy, she's not particularly good, but boy is she fast."

THE ZOO AT BCSP

THERE WAS A zoo near our house, in the park, but not to be pictured as a zoo exists today. If it were to be compared, the park service and Dad would have to be imprisoned for animal cruelty. It was a large square building with cages each about 12' x 12', with concrete floors. It contained mostly local animals, though there was a bear named Old Joe along with two or three other bears, and a buffalo enclosed in a sagging wire farm fence. Ronnie and I would torment the old, wooly buffalo, until he charged the fence, and it would bend way down. Then we would run off imagining it was going to get us. Actually he could have trampled us, if that bend fence ever caved in.,

There were the local black bears. One won Old Joe, who would sit slumped in the corner of his cage. I don't know how old he was, or how long confined in the horrid square cage. Dad did have concern for him. I remember he would go down there to talk quietly to the him and go into the cage to feed him treats. It may not have been bravery, as I considered it then, because I suspect now that there was no danger; the sad bear's spirit was broken. There were a couple of other bears, because dad got a scare by one, while was cleaning their pens.

While in Dad's office one day, I heard a frantic person

report that Old Joe was not in his cage, but out with the public. It was a busy day. I watched Dad get up, reach in a drawer, get a gun and a giant Hershey bar. (He always kept those Hershey bars stashed for easy access for himself). He headed straight for the zoo, and I followed him. There was a crowd surrounding an overweight woman, who was standing, arms up rigid with fright, while Old Joe was sniffing her belly. Dad quietly walked up to the bear, began quietly talking to him, opened the candy bar, gave Joe a sniff and began slowly walking back to the cages with Old Joe following.

We kids brought raisins and other treats down to the cage. Joe would stick his tongue through the steel mesh fence and we would give him goodies he liked to eat. Then one evening, some sub-human cut an inch of Joe's tongue off; Seemingly while he had it through the cage enclosure seeking a treat. Someone found it on the ground outside the cage, with old Joe seated, slumped in the corner. We were horrified and sickened. The story appeared in the Indianapolis newspaper. No culprit was discovered.

There were snakes, including poisonous ones. Occasionally, if we had a lot of *public* on hand, Dad would enter the snake room, pin a rattlesnake, then grasp it behind its head, hold it with its fangs hooked on the edge of a glass container. I don't know how he stimulated it to release its venom into the glass container, but that is what is meant to "milk" a poisonous snake. I certainly was impressed. He was my brave dad.

As you might imagine, this is dangerous, but life-saving business. The venom extracted is what make the anti-venom used to save a life when a victim of a poisonous snake bite is brought to the emergency room of a hospital. However, it should not be done by an amateur; it's dangerous. There are those, who are trained herpologist that do this work in a lab under controlled conditions. I'm sure there are other skilled snake handlers,who know how to do this procedure, but it's not smart for someone, who want to show off, to do this. In the case of my father, eighty years ago, he was an outdoorsman, and a conservationist in spirit and job, so that's the explanation for his doing the "milking."

At another time a male employee tried the same thing with a copperhead, and got bitten. The frightened man came to the office with two puncture wounds on one hand. Dad calmly got out a sharp knife and ordered me out of the office. The procedure for snake bites then, was to make a cut into the bite site. The purpose was to 'bleed out the poison." That's not the accepted practice now. In fact, it's a myth. Don't even think it.

Later when we moved to Florida, we learned of a herpetologist named Ross Allen, who went in search of poisonous snakes for the purpose of "milking" them. His efforts were to provide venom for development of anti-venom. It might interest some readers, that the author, Marjorie Kinnon Rawlings, the Pulitzer Prize winning novelist, who wrote The Yearling knew Ross Allen. In her memoir, she wrote about going out at night to hunt rattle snakes with him. She was a Yankee who had purchased an orange grove in Central Florida. So she lived and wrote in rural Florida, a little before and during the time we had moved there. She would have had to contend with snakes where she lived, and wanted to overcome her fear of them. Her reasoning was sound. I own her books, all of them, and reread them many times with enjoyment.

She also came to Florida with racial biases, which she did not at first even recognize. That is understandable given her time and place. One of skills as a writer, was her ability to accept and admire the differences in the people with him she was living. As she wrote about the local people, and got to know them, she realized she did have racial issues she needed to overcome. It is commendable that she could acknowledge that and do something about it.

Wherever we lived after leaving Chicago, until grown, we had to be aware of snakes. Dad made certain that we could recognize the few snakes that were venomous. That left us free to touch or pick us harmless ones. I had played with a black snake enough, so that it became quite tame. I would let it hang around my neck and wiggle into my shirt and around my body or come out a sleeve. With it on my person, I would deliberately go down to where there was public, to watch their reactions to a little girl with a black snake crawling out her armpit.

Dad did allow and tolerate our making **pets** out of any animal except dangerous ones, however he didn't want them in the house. One day to our surprise a little screech owl flew onto our kitchen table as we were eating, and stopped right in front of Dad. He nonchalantly offered it a bite to eat as if that were an everyday occurrence. Mother was quite startled as we all were. It seemed that Dad had been feeding it by hand down at the animal cages, so had brought it up to the house to be funny. Screech owls are so dear.

After the war ended, many veterans came into the park, some in large bus loads. Many were the walking wounded. I was stunned by the shock of seeing these soldiers maimed and crippled. There was one fellow whose entire head was bandaged with holes for his eyes and mouth. The most we understood about that war, was when we were reminded that there was a war in Europe,and that was why we needed to eat all our supper. One of my step brothers came back with what was then called "shell shock," which is now termed Post Traumatic Stress Disorder (PTSD). We kids knew very little about the chaos and horror of war waged in Europe. Years later we learned about the holocaust, when we studied history at FSU in the late 1950s. It seems incredible that two world wars, along with the horror of the holocaust took place in the middle of Christendom.

THE MEAD FAMILY AND WALT DISNEY

T HERE WAS A movie made in the late 1940's called "So Dear to my Heart". From Wikipedia when making a search for, **So Dear to My Heart,** I've taken the following excerpt:

"Midnight and Jeremiah

Midnight and Jeremiah is a 1943 children's book written by Sterling North and illustrated by Kurt Wiese. It concerns a boy named Jeremiah who adopts a black baby lamb and as the story progresses, they share a strong bond. Midnight and Jeremiah was the basis for the 1948 film So Dear to My Heart, whose title was used for a movie called So Dear To My heart.

So Dear To My **Heart** is a story of emotional depth and beauty filled with the gaiety, songs, dances, and color of Indiana in the early days of the century. Saturday Review wrote: "The story rings with music; it is itself a kind of prose ballad of backwoods Indiana, merry with a gnarly humor" everywhere

Since the setting for the book was in Indiana farm country, it is understandable why Disney chose beautiful Brown County. It followed, why not in the State Park? Why not the Mead kids?

There came a day when Daddy took a backroom of our house, built twelve little stalls into it, with a place at the head of each stall for a baby bottle to be inserted to feed twelve little lambs. One exciting day twelve baby lambs were delivered, and we kids were told they were ours to play with, hold, feed and make spoiled babies of them. What bliss. And one of them was to be trained to be a naughty little lamb, named Midnight. And guess who got to baby and train that lamb? Byron, of course. His lamb had a distinctive black face, was very clever and in short order, would follow Byron where ever he walked. Mine was named Bobby and I would hold him in my arms and rock him in a rocking chair. I'm pictured in an Indianapolis newspaper holding him in the rocking chair along with Molly and Ronnie holding their lambs.

Eventually, a write up with pictures of Molly and Byron interacting with the lambs, appeared in an issue of Life Magazine in 1946. There were representatives and photographers from Disney and newspapers milling about our home for weeks. In the end there was so much delay getting the movie started that our lambs outgrew the role and could not be used, so the whole movie was moved elsewhere including the filming. The movie, So Dear to My Heart, when released was a big hit.

I don't remember being disappointed. The lambs were what was big in our minds. Probably Mother, Dad and Byron would have liked to see it through. Mother got a call telling her my picture was going to be on the cover of Life and gave the month. When we went to buy the magazine, it was something or someone else. To me it was the thrill of the baby lambs. How many kids gets a dozen baby lambs handed to them to spoil? Mother's scrapbook has letters to and from Disney executives and the contract for Byron, who was paid a nice sum for training the lambs

Herding animals, like sheep and goats, can make such neat pets. When my children were about the same age, as we were at the Disney time in Indiana, someone gave us an angora goat. It was made a pet when it was a baby by a family of children. His name was Sam. He was such a precious animal. I could sit in a lawn chair, turn him on his back on my lap, all four hoofs straight up skyward, his long ears flapped back, and he would be in a state of bliss. As long as he had our attention, he was content. When the children ran and played, Sam would be cavorting happily among them, bounding here and there. When the children were in school, he would wander about looking for his playmates. When I was Inside, I would hear a tap, tap, and it would be Sam with hoofs on the window sill, trying to look in. Other times he butted the door to get me outside with him. I jogged back then, and when I would jog, Sam jogged also, and stayed right behind me—Never straying. So if I jogged along the side of a road, and a car passed, I could count on taillights coming on shortly after the car was by me. I was sure they were thinking, *was that a goat chasing that middle age woman?*

A grocery store close by us had a grand opening, so my children grabbed their bikes to join the opening with Sam bouncing along beside them. They dumped their bikes, went into the store leaving Sam outside. He trotted up to the door to check on his buddies, tripped the electric eye of the door, and trotted right in and headed straight to the produce department. The children came home breathless with excitement, and told me the new manager got quite hostile. With their eye opened wide, they said, "He even cussed, Mama!"

Now in reminiscing, Sam's name might come up and there will be a shift in tone to a soft moan, "Oh, Sam, dear Sam. What a wonderful boy he was." We had to give him up. We had a farm fence around our property with a gate that opened to the side to our neighbors. Our neighbors were very elderly, and had a scant number of flowers around their patio. Sam was very aware of those flowers. If the children carelessly left a gate open, Sam made a dash for those few flowers. He would pluck them running and dash back home through the gate. The neighbor was a gentleman and kind to our children, even Kevin, my hyperactive son and Sam, the goat. One day he came to my door, and apologetically announced to me, "Dawn, either that goat goes, or we do." I had no choice; The goat was given to a kindly farmer. Kevin, we kept. Since this was Florida, the neighbor had devised a way to keep Kevin at bay. If Kevin outstayed his welcome, he got a soft spray down with a garden hose.

We did have a sheep that did not work out so well, but that was all my fault. My ex-husband was neglecting yard work. Sam was not a grass eater. He preferred the neighbor's flowers and other store-bought stuff. I decided I'd import a sheep to mow the lawn. I consulted the want ads in the newspaper under the heading of livestock. A man, who answered my call, told me he had some lambs just a few weeks old. Oh, boy. I got a price and commitment. Before hanging up, he says, "Mam, you do understand that my sheep are Barbados sheep?" Here's another instance of my lack of self-control. Barbados? I was not going for a type of wool; I was after another pet and a live lawn mower. Though I did about mountain sheep, it didn't register at this time.

So I gathered a close friend of mine, and our son, Kevin, into our station wagon and drove out to a very rural area to get my sheep. The man came out of the barn, carrying a darling little brown "sheep" that looked just like Bambi, Disney's deer. I was startled. The visual I was holding in my head was of a little lamb like we had in our Disney days, however he was so cute, that I didn't hesitate to complete the purchase. The man assured me he loved grass. I had eleven-year-old Kevin, climb into the cargo compartment of the station wagon and he eagerly complied, holding out his arms, so happy to be a part of this special event. As the man approached the car, the lamb was putting up a mighty struggle. I'm thinking, that critter needs to be tamed down. In he went and down goes Kevin, then down went Bambi. It was a mighty struggle. The friend and I raced for the front seats, and off we went. From the rear of the car, we could hear literally crashing and banging. I was somewhat concerned it might leap the seats and get to the front. Every once in a while, Kevin would holler reassurances. "I got him, Mama. I got him, don't worry." When we got home and parked, I ordered, "Don't open the door until I get the gate shut."

When I opened the car cargo door, Bambi sailed out and bounce, bounce like a beautiful gazelle, he sailed away, around the house and back again. We all really loved him except the EX. He did tame down for a while, and the children could enjoy him, and he enjoyed the grass. Then one day, Mother came to visit. While sitting in a lawn chair and watching the children, she called me to her side to "alert me", she said. By then, Bambi didn't bounce, he strutted. Making an effort to be subtle, she pointed to his male attachments. They were not subtle. That was her alert. "Dawnie, I think this animal might become dangerous." It was not an exaggerated statement. I took note.

In the meantime, Bambi had begun harassing the neutered Sam, who was getting more than annoyed. He was highly distressed. Once, to give dear Sam some relief from Bambi's constant harassment, I tied the goat outside the fence, shut the gate and started to the house. Suddenly I heard some earth-shaking thumps behind me. It was Bambi in an attack mode. I swung around just in time to grab his horns; yell stop and sock him unintentionally in the eye. He stopped, blinking and shaking his head. Happily, I had control of him from then on by facing him and shouting STOP.

A short time later, we were having an outdoor cookout and Kevin decided the guests needed a circus performance, so he put his sister, Anna, on Bambi's back, who charged off a short distance, and scraped her off on an orange tree. She was furious.

More and more unpleasant incidents occurred. One afternoon I was showering and the bathroom door opened and Kevin's voice reported, "Bambi butted me into the fence post, and knocked me out!" Less than a minute later, the shower curtain ripped open, and little sister, Anna hollered, "He's just being dramatic, Mama. He wasn't knocked out."

I had noticed that Bambi was running toward our shop door out back where his food was kept, and leaping to slam it with his head. The noise of his head hitting the door was huge. That was when he wished to alert us that he was hungry. Soon my EX was concerned about going out to his shop. I would see him at the back door, checking for a sight of Bambi, then step out and make a wild, dash for the shop.

So now Bambi had to go. The same farmer, who given Sam at nice home, came to get him. Sometime later, I called to see how Bambi and Sam were doing. His reply was, "Lady, have you ever seen a cross between a duck and a Barbados sheep?" Now what did he mean by that? We passed that farmyard one day and the kids saw Bambi standing atop a hay stack overlooking his kingdom. He looked magnificent.

A FLORIDA VACATION

WHILE STILL IN the park one year, our parents offered us an option. Would we like to have a Christmas at home with presents or go to Florida with camping during the holidays. We definitely opted for Florida.

The trip down was memorable for many reasons. The car was jammed packed with snuggly with four kids in the back seat, and one who got car sick. We also pulled a little cargo trailer behind stuffed full of camping equipment, bedding, food—enough supplies for a week. Molly and I sang. We all did a fine job singing with, "Ninety bottles of beer on a wall…" and other songs. With four kids in the backseat of a chevy sedan, there were disagreements. This was long before seat belts, so we were usually bouncing around, wanting to know when we would ever get there.

Dad held the opinion that all the gas stations bathrooms in the state of Georgia were locked for our protection, So if a bathroom call rang out, Dad would turn and say to the boys, "Well sons, time to change a tire." With that, he pulled to side of the road and the boys would smugly (I thought) get out to go to the back of the car, Dad would raise the trunk, to get out a jack or tire and the rest of the bathroom break just got done right by the car. Now for the girls, things got more complicated. That took driving along searching for an area that could be accessed for privacy. When found there were shouts of relief, so we girl would traverse into woods or a bushy area where we could find a hiding place and squat.

Once down south, all four windows would be wide open. Hair and loose objects would fly and dispositions flared in the heat. Another feature of a car ride with him was his smoking pipe. Every so often, he had to dump his old ashes out and refill. What did he do? He held the pipe out the window, and tapped it on the side of car door. With all windows opened, dead ashes along with live ones, would fly out and right back into the rear window and in amongst us kids. It kept us alert. One other travel memory we laugh about was his method for keeping order. He kept a small, child's toy broom in the front seat on the floor beside him for easy grabbing. It was about three feet long. If there arose any fighting in the backset, Dad would grab that handy broom and flap it over his shoulder. It didn't matter on whom it landed. It was indiscriminate, and it did bring order.

Mother was the official navigator, and would have maps spread out on her lap. We could hear such instructions such as, "Now at the next intersection, we'll be taking route such and such. Then suddenly. We'd hear, "Oh, Hansel, there's another route here, that goes. . .",

Dad would have to say, "We're at an intersection, Peggy. I have to know." The car then was parked and he consulted the maps.

Then there were the Burma Shave signs. We all came to alert when a new series of those signs were spotted. They were a series of signs by the road side, each with a line usually rhyming with the one before or next, ending with a big Burma Shave sign. The first to spot one hollered out, "Burma Shave signs coming up!!" Fights and arguments broke up, as we all jumped to attention, to shout out each sign as it flashed by.

We were headed to the Ocala National Forest where there were springs. Springs in Florida are so beautiful, crystal clear and deep. Some look bottomless, the walls lined with caves. In a large one, thousands of gallons of cool, clear water are bubbling up continuously. All that water has to go somewhere so there is a strong clear stream that flows from the spring, usually to a larger stream and eventually to a river. In Florida there are many of these preserved in parks, recreational areas or just very scenic areas. In the parks, they are enjoyed for swimming, snorkeling, scuba diving and manatee habitats among other wildlife. All of the Ocala National Forest is made up of a dense, jungle-like forest surrounding several springs. While the beaches in Florida are so commercialized and crowded, the springs are for the most part kept in their natural state with abundant wildlife that you might not see anywhere else. The are deer, otters, raccoons along with other wildlife on the spring run off meandering through the thick forest. To me, the springs are the best part of Florida.

I remember an occasion when Mother was painting at a spring deep in the woods. While she painted, we were climbing up a tree, crawling out on a limb and jumping into a small spring bubbling up amongst some rocks. Our aim had to be good, or we could be injured on the rocks. Mother was busy painting the scene, and oblivious that we were risking life and limb off the tree. Every once in a while, she would call out asking, "Is everything all right?" and we would assure her that all was fine.

There was a large spring in a park south of Tallahassee called Wakulla Springs, that had a very high diving board that had a long ladder straight up the side. The water was so clear, we could see caves down deep and lots of fish. Around the outside, clear of the spring, alligators swam about. They rarely go in the spring area itself, as they don't like the cold water from the spring. We didn't worry about them; it was a mutual respect situation. When you jumped off that diving tower, first there was the "wedgie", then the rapid descent down, down into the cold water. As the downward momentum slowed, the person would then feel the spring water ascending to stop your momentum and push you rapidly to the surface. It was great fun. As adults, Byron and

I, visited there when the high dive tower was still in place. Once we were up there, we were afraid to jump and then realized,we were afraid to go back down that ladder. I have to tell that brave Molly would have gone off that board in a pretty dive. That diving tower as it was then, does not exist, but a very safe zig, zag structure is in place. Throughout the years performers both brave souls and professionals have done some skillful diving off that high dive. That recreational park has a very, fine hotel there to this day.

A JUNIPER SPRINGS CANOE TRIP

T HIS TRIP WAS our first time in Florida as well as camping. We camped in a tent at Juniper Springs, a rustic park within the Ocala National Forest in central Florida. The spring was and still is contained in a large, rock lined basin, built long before we visited there in the 1940's. Set above the basin at the spring was and is an old Mill House, with a water wheel churning continuously, from the force of the water bubbling up from the spring. The stream created by the springs, is a clear creek with a gentle current.

There is a four-hour canoe trip down the run ending in a river where there has to be a pre-arrangement for pickup get back to the campsite at the end. The clear stream begins shallow, but as it nears the river it widens out, deepens and the canoers have to watch carefully to keep track of the current so not to end in an alligator run, or stuck in the sawgrass and water hyacinths. If that happens, one might have to climb out of the canoe, backtrack and be skillful enough to get back into the canoe without flipping it over. That is how it was then and as it is now.

I will describe it as it would be to us kids then, because we were visiting Florida for the first time from Indiana. Everything about it was new to us. We had two canoes, so there was three of us in each canoe. We were downright ignorant about canoes and the trip ahead of us. What an adventure! We barely got a few feet down the clear stream, when we were halted by a fallen tree. We had to push the canoes under, climb over and get back in without flipping the canoe. Forget staying dry. Because of the push of the springs, the water is gently rolling us along carrying the canoe, but it takes a little time to learn to keep the canoe on course. The person in the stern does most of the steering, while the person in the front helps and also uses his paddle to maintain the canoe keeping it in the stream. On that run both paddlers are busy not only paddling, but trying to keep the canoe away from the edge of the run, or out of the bushes or caught on fallen logs. Sometimes, as we went around corners, the back of the canoe would sweep gently toward the bank. On occasion there would be a large alligator lying down the bank with it its huge head not a few feet away from stern of the canoe. If a alligator was in the water as the canoe approached, it simply sank and the canoe slid quietly over it. About two hours into the run, there was a small platform built where we could park the canoe, have a snack and empty bladders in the bushes or may take a swim to cool off. By the time we got that far we had become fairly competent canoers, but how we avoided a mishap is amazing. In the end, when we reached the river, we pulled up to the sandy shore next to some bushes. The front two in dad's canoe stepped out hurriedly into the shallow water. This left his canoe to swing back into the bushes. Now the front outweighed, lifted up and caused the back to sink with the overweight daddy down into the water. When Mother discovered that Dad was in trouble, and almost out of sight, she called anxiously, "Oh, Hansel, are you alright?"

Dad called back reassuringly, "I'm right here, Peggy, safe in the honeysuckle bushes."

Since then, all through the years, we, with our children, nieces and nephews, grandchildren have continued to go down that run. I would like I give it another go before I die, but that's doubtful. If Ronnie were still alive, he'd see to it that I'd have one last go.

Juniper Spring with the run is still an adventure—Still in its natural state. Now there's kayaks going up and down it along with the canoes. When my children were little, I spoke with a ranger about alligators and was told that they had never had an incident involving any wildlife. That was then. Tourists in parks today, don't behave themselves. They feed wild life, or torment them. Let me assure you that I'm certainly fearful of alligators now. So much of their natural habitat in Florida has been corrupted. During breeding and egg laying season, the poor gators are confused. Some ancient voice says to a lady alligator, "Go west mama gator, lay some eggs, …." And off she goes and runs straight into a garage door.

Other years we vacationed at Homosassa Springs and Chrystal River along the gulf coast of Florida. These were wonderful fishing, boating and swimming vacations. These spring are also manatee habitats. I live now in Tennessee and am amazed at the folks here, who go regularly to Florida and are ignorant of the springs, parks and the national forests in the interior.

One year my husband and myself took two Bostonians down the Juniper run. They were new to springs, canoes, wildlife and the outdoors in general. She had been trained as an opera singer and he was a professional pianist. We had things arranged for that trip, for him to be in the front of my canoe. She was in another and seated in the middle. Far down the stream, the pianist and I lost sight of the other canoe, but we could hear her lovely voice singing happily as they meandered down the stream. As we came down toward the end of the trip, the water had widened out considerably and I lost the current, and we came to a halt in thick grass.

"Well," I said. "I'm going have to get out of this thing and get us out of here." He looked startled, but to my surprise, that Yankee climbed out as well, into neck deep water. We pushed the canoe backwards out to the main current and managed to get back in without a spill.

When we were on our way headed down to the river, I mentioned to him, "That may have been a gator run that got us off course."

He turned to me, his eyes opened wide. "Really?" he asked.

When we came to the end at a river, there was his wife

waving happily, but obviously concerned about him. He had been having dangerously, high blood-pressure problems, and we were later than the others getting down to join them. They were eagerly looking for us. He got within hearing distance, and shouted, "Oh, Honey, I've had the most wonderful experience of my whole life! I've been in an alligator run."

Another time we had a small boy with us seated in the floor of the canoe. He had overheard conversations regarding the wildlife we might encounter. So as we pushed off, "He cupped his mouth with his hands and hollered very loudly, "Alligators, we come in peace!"

⌐

Brown County State Park did provide our father a challenge, for which he was well equipped. He was completely involved with every aspect of the park and saw it as a service to the community, state and country. Once again, Mother put forth all her talents to be a support for him and loving mother to us. What an experience it was to have available to us, a home in a beautiful environment, be part of the conservation of wildlife and be free to explore and grow as individuals.

After Brown County we moved to Florida in 1948. Why? Neither Byron nor I remember an explanation given for a move. It could have happened, because of some problems we experienced, while we were still in the park. The park had a summer home for the governor, his family and guests. Molly remembered politicians and drinking. It was very hard time for Mother, though she never spoke of it. Byron and his dad were very much alike and devoted to each other. So he must have been anxious, when Mother packed us up for a trip back to Chicago. I remember that as a visit to the cousins' home, where we stayed for a brief time. Apparently promises were made and kept. We were together again as a strong family heading for new way of life.

Another reason for our move might have been dad's health. His heart was a big undercurrent in our life. I remember he took frequent naps needing to rest. When we left him to go to town, Mother would seem anxious. Without her realizing it, she would say frequently, "We need to hurry now. We need to get home to your father." He had had rheumatic fever as a child. Though he recovered, he was left with a severely damaged heart valve. When we hugged him with an ear to his chest, we could hear his heart pump, with an ominous *whoosh* sound. From the time of his recovery as a child, Dad constantly carried with him the knowledge that this defect could cause his death. He never complained, nor did he seem in anyway reduced by it. Actually he refused to be reduced by it. He was a hard worker, and accomplished much throughout his life. Our next move was to an old CCC camp in the middle of the Apalachicola National Forest. Whatever he had been hired to do in regards to that move, he achieved and more.

M DAWN DAYTON

THE MEADS IN THE APALACHICOLA NATIONAL FOREST

I WAS ABOUT TWELVE-YEARS-OLD, when we made our next move to a national forest tucked just in the Florida panhandle on the southwestern side of Tallahassee, Florida. At about 570,000 acres, it's the state's largest national forest, extending west into the panhandle and south to the gulf coast. Dad was given the opportunity to take over an old CCC camp in that forest and develop it into a recreational area for the county and city of Tallahassee.

I consulted Wikipedia for information regarding these CCC camps and learned as follows:

> The CCC camps The **Civilian Conservation Corps (CCC)** was a government work relief program that ran from 1933 to 1942 in the United States. The CCC was a major part of President Roosevelt's New Deal to supply manual labor jobs for the unemployed. At the same time gave development and preservation of natural resources in rural lands owned by federal, state, and local governments. The CCC was designed to supply jobs for young men and to relieve families

who had difficulty finding jobs during the great
depression in the United States.

We had been hired to develop a recreational area in that forest at the site of two small, beautiful, spring-fed lakes. I can't find much on-line regarding this particular remote CCC camp, but it still physically existed when we arrived there, but had long been abandoned. The Tallahassee Elks Club got the smart idea to develop the old camp into a recreational area for the use of the residents of Tallahassee and Leon County. We accomplished that and more. Through the years since, we've had such pleasure in relating stories of many, experiences of our time there.

Our goal was to make this available for visitors to come to the silver lake primarily to swim off the white sand beach, and to picnic at tables scattered in the wooded acres. Dispersed throughout the area, were the sixteen very rustic, one-room unfinished cabins used by the workers while the CCC camp was in operation. Today, they would be advertised as primitive, very much so. Each cabin had nothing but six bunk beds left over from the old CCC days. If these cabins were compared these days to facilities in state and national parks, they would have to be promoted as very primitive. That is the only adjective to describe them. However, once we got the park going, they were continually in use.

AN OLD CCC CAMP TO SILVER
LAKE RECREATIONAL AREA

I WILL ATTEMPT TO give you a visual of the potential presented there. Silver Lake was an area of about fifty-six acres cut out of the of the national forest. The small main lake was, spring-fed with a cleared beach, and was surrounded by forest. That lake was joined to another smaller one by a swampy, snaky area, crowded with cypress trees with their knees protruding from the water and alligators. To go from one lake to the other we had to canoe or pole our way through. A row boat would get stuck in it. Both lakes invited fishing, row boats and canoeing . Nine of the cabins faced one lake or the other. The last four were set off more remotely.

Throughout the camp, there were big old oak trees, draped with Spanish moss, cypress groves, palmetto fronds, a hardwood hammock and pine woods. The sixteen cabins in groups of four were set throughout the wooded area. There were two bath houses with toilets and showers to serve sixteen cabins and the day users. One of these served primarily cabin campers and the other cabins and day-use public. Up near the entrance were two larger four-room cabins, with kitchens and porch, upgraded to rustic, because these two had a bathroom in each. Molly and I with our parents in one, with Ronnie and Byron in the other. These apparently were the officer's quarters for the original camp. These two, very rustic cabins together, became what it took to give us a home for our family. Surrounding this acerage was a fence with an entrance gate that could be locked at night. Not far from our houses was a hut that served to collect entrance fees for daily visitors and an office. It was for us, roughing it.

In middle of the grounds was a very large mess-hall with large dining area and kitchen for feeding a the CCC workers. There was one small building convenient to the mess hall and swimming area that became our concession stand. Any possible spaces that allowed for it, became campground, ballfield and picnic areas. This was what was there when we arrived. Actually, it was all either primitive or rustic according to the eyes of the beholder. In the eyes of those who love the outdoors, it was beautiful, and to Dad it was loaded with potential. It took about a year of work to get ready for the *public*. From the time of our arrival and it opened for public use, there was endless work in improvement. Ronnie, by this time, had reached an age to be able to lifeguard, do repairs, and man the concession stands. Ronnie and I were very much part of the workforce.

Probably, the docks had to be built and or improved, upon and on them was added a lifeguard perch and diving boards. The smaller building near the lake became a concession stand, with pavilion Dad built attached to it. Later, a juke box was installed there and a ping pong table. Close by was horseshoe court. Dirt paths ran everywhere. There was a field with a baseball diamond. Eventually there was a camping area for tents, and trailer campers. The emphasis in the beginning was to attract day-use people in order to have an income.

When we arrived, I was finishing up the seventh grade, so must have been close to thirteen-years-old. Byron, with all his past responsibilities on the farm, and in Brown County became Dad's right-hand man in construction and maintenance. Of course, Mother threw herself into working wherever she was needed, as she always had. The rest of us weren't babied, so worked where or on whatever we were capable or were needed. It became a family enterprise. That meant no specialized labor. *As needed* meant, collecting entrance fees, cleaning bathhouses and concession stand, picking up paper and trash, selling at the concessions stand, lifeguarding, placing campers, fixing meals, repairs and the never ending needs of the public. During peak time, this meant twelve hour days.

By this time, we kids were emerging into distinct personalities. We were all good students. Byron was very serious, hardworking with Dad and as a student. Molly, very pretty, began to be very serious about her looks, boys and being accepted by her peers. Bless her heart, Silver Lake didn't offer much to fulfill those needs. However, once the public started coming during the summers, she had her share of boys and friends. Ronnie enjoyed it most when the place was full people. He worked as directed or persuaded under Dad, Byron and Mother. I loved the place, with varmints, swimming, and canoeing. I do not remember thinking of those summers as laborious. It was our life for that season. And in the "off" time during the cold season, it was school, reading and tranquility.

Since, both Mother and Dad were always occupied outside the home in park work, housekeeping or house beautiful could not be a focus, especially so at Silver Lake. Our *home(s)* did not even have much potential for beautifying. Mother being humorous, once shared with me, "One can't keep a perfect house and be an intellectual. Well I've chosen to be an intellectual." I can see the wisdom in that philosophy. That house philosophy served us well in those pitiful officers' quarters. Our house and the one close by, was pine wood, unfinished, with a small, screened front porch with a table, chairs and daybed used as a couch. It was almost camping.

This front porch, rustic at best, was a sort of social center, rather like a family kitchen in most homes. Business was conducted there. Friendly public might wonder up and decide to visit awhile. Homesick children, attending camp, were sent up to our porch, where I rocked them to a sleepy state and convinced them they really could survive the night away from home. We joked, that our humble table welcomed alligator hunters one day, and college professors the next. That was so true and how great was that?

We were about a year there at Silver Lake before opening up for the public's use. All the buildings had to be put in working order, and new construction done. There were the empty, primitive cabins. The mess hall and kitchen were just left, as they were when the CCC camp closed some years earlier. Now this facility was updated from a small army base, to reopen as a recreational area to attract the residents Tallahassee and Leon County. It entailed a lot of construction and purchases.

From professional photos of us kids in Chicago, it appeared we were then dressed in satin and velveteen. Mother and Dad lived well there. At Silver Lake very few photos were taken. I know we went barefooted, and barelegged weather permitting. The only time we wore dresses was for school, which were required. There was never, ever distress or frustration expressed about our financial situation. We knew we had to accumulate enough money in the summer months to tide us through the fall, winter and spring. Money was tight. It was accepted and we had to work hard to surmount the setback. That was it.

Mother and Dad had their start during the great depression. All four of us kids were born during this same time period. Dad told us that the people who threw themselves out of the windows in Chicago and New York were people who didn't own the door knobs on their door. It was all on paper, meaning credit. I think Dad did some financial advising during that time they lived in Chicago. They were very frugal, all to avoid debt. I don't remember any feelings of deprivation. We had not been exposed to "keeping up with the Joneses" mentality. It was our life style. One didn't buy a car on time. One bought a car with cash, then began to put money away for the next one.

We once had a car that was being kept together with sheer determination by dad and Byron. One very, rainy-day Byron drove me to high school. The front passenger side windows of our cars then, had one large window, and beside that a wing window that twisted inward on a hinge. That day, hanging from the rearview mirror and near my feet was a jug. It contained gasoline, because the fuel pump for the car was out of commission and he was to get a new one. It had a hose that went out the little, flap passenger window to under the hood. Also, the windshield wipers were nonoperational. So, there was a string attached to his side of the wipers and a string to mine and we alternated pulling the string to keep the windshield clear. By the time we got to school, I was laughing uproariously and Byron was grinning so pleased at my enjoyment of his innovations. He dropped me off right in front of the school.

One of our first purchases were empty steel drums. Mother

was sent to town to fetch a trailer loaded with of a bunch of 55-gallon drums. On the return home, after entering the forest, and driving down our secluded forest road, she was stopped by some well-dressed men and questioned about those drums. It turned out they were revenuers suspicious that she was hauling the drums for a moonshine enterprise in the national forest. That certainly didn't jibe with the young women that departed Chicago. Mother might have known about moonshiners from her reading, but that certainly wouldn't have entered her head when she was stopped. It might have gone like this:

"Mam, do you know why we stopped you?

Mother, politely, curiously, "No, is there a problem? I'm Peggy Mead. And you?"

"We are Federal Agents, mam.'"

"Oh, my, are you lost?"

She herself, was out of her element in these acres and acres of heavily wooded forest off the only paved road. It must have dawned on these revenuers that something was *off.* She didn't fit the mold. Rather than being nervous or defensive, she would have projected an attitude of helpfulness and curiosity. I recall when she got home, she was so tickled with that happening. She had been suspected of transporting something in connection with moonshine, of all things. She was an interesting letter writer—I'm sure details of that encounter went into a letter back home.

One use for the drums were to set all them around the park as trash cans. We soon learned to be dismayed, when a group at a picnic shelter was having watermelon. Can you imagine a 55-gallon tub, full of watermelon rinds and flies in hot Florida summers? We had to a empty these containers and dispose of the contents at the end of a long day.

YOU MUST NOT LOSE CONTROL OF THE BEACH

T HE PRIORITY FOR development was with a white sand beach bordered by two docks. On one dock Dad built a diving board about twelve feet high and a low one off to one side. On the high diving board stand, was the life guard perch. Off the swimming area we had row boats and canoes for rental. Also here were large tractor innertubes to play on in the water.

Early on we all, except Dad, took the Red Cross life guard course to be certified as life guards. That course included being able to save someone drowning, if you saw the need, but you were fully clothed. We came prepared for the lesson, clothes over our bathing suits. We thought it hilarious when our mother came running down the beach stripping off pieces of clothing and submerging to remove shoes and then swim out for a rescue. She was in her early forties then, but to us she was over the hill. A friend of mine, named Lecky from school, who loved Silver Lake took the course with us. She along with other young friends from school, worked with us during peak times each summer.

I think it's nothing short of a miracle that we never lost a swimmer. We did have one serious incident. This occurred at a time when Byron had tumor removed from the inside of his thigh, that entailed a heavy cast on his leg. He was down at the beach when Molly had to have a brief break from the lifeguard perch, so Byron relieved her. No sooner did he get on the lifeguard perch when he thought he saw a little face disappear about 125 feet away near the other dock. Uneasy, he dived off the perch, and swam over to the area where he thought he had seen the child's face. There was a woman in the vicinity, and he asked her if she had seen a little girl. She said she hadn't seen anything. He, however, began to dive under to explore at the drop off. Where the water was deep, it got weedy, so he began to run his hands through the weeds. Sure enough, he encountered a little girl about eight or nine lying on the bottom in the weeds. He managed to get her to the dock, but was handicapped by the cast on his leg and couldn't get her up on the dock. A man was mowing not far away, saw what was going on, and he rushed down and assisted him. On the dock Byron performed artificial respiration on the girl and she revived. The cast had to be replaced.

There was a sudden drop off at the swimming area, so Dad had situated the life guard perch and high dive right at this area. At times, we did have occasional difficulties in the swimming area. I had problems, because I was skinny and never looked my age The swimmers didn't always take me seriously, especially students from FSU. Dad commanded us very seriously, "You must not lose control of the beach."

Byron could hold his breath long enough to swim under water all the way between docks. He also enjoyed floating face down, slowly sink under without causing a ripple of water, to reappear a long way away or come up under a dock. Unintentionally on his part, the float and sink looked somewhat like an alligator floating and disappearing. One drizzly day, he was having a solo swim. From up at the picnic shelter, a lady spied what appeared as a head, disappear and then not reappear. It was puzzling, and she was concerned it might be a child. The more she thought about it, the more she became very anxious, so she rushed down to the lake, hiked her dress to her waist, and waded in calling for help. By then, Byron had emerged from under a dock, and hearing her panic, he too became alarmed. So a diligent, but fruitless, search was underway, with repeated dives along the drop off where the head was last seen, until it dawned on hm that he was searching for himself. He, a shy teenager, had to explain to the lady clutching her wet skirt, that she wasn't mistaken about the disappearance of the head, because he was it. Later in telling, he felt rather bad for the lady.

A few hundred feet from shore. Byron had built a raft on top of several empty steel 55-gallon drums. A real draw to test your swimming skills, but could be an annoyance for the lifeguard. Young males couldn't resist standing on the edge of that raft and rocking it. If it happened to flip, it could knock a person's brains out. Once a few male FSU students were rocking the raft having a high old time, so I tooted my whistle, hollering to them, "Stop rocking the raft, please. It might flip." There was a pause, the boys looked at me, saw what looked like a kid, then commenced rocking again, only harder. *What to do?* Dad was in the gatehouse too far away to help or advise. He would want this stopped. I was in a dilemma. Finally, I dove in, swam underwater to the raft, climbed up, lunged, tackling the nearest boy, landing us both in the water—I sunk him and held him there. The girl from the lifeguard perch didn't look like much more than a kid, but could hold her breath a long time, and was at home in the water. The incident got reported to the owner at the gate house, who happened to be my dad, so all was well. I got control of the beach, even if my method was not in any lifeguard certification manual.

Some girls had a row boat in the swimming area. A rowboat was heavy and bulky, which the girl with the oars was having trouble handling. When I requested them to move it, I explained that the rowboat was too big and heavy and posed a danger to the swimmers. One girl called me a hick and had a laugh with her friends. They were right about the hick. In my mind, they were silly, prissy girls, with flowered bathing caps. For some reason, the flowered bathing caps annoyed me. I was well aware that I lacked the appearance of someone in charge of the crowded beach. They did move the boat, but with insolence.

Another frequent minor annoyance, was watching a swimmer struggling to make it to the raft, climb on, beckon to a friend still standing in neck-deep water in front of the drop off and holler, "Come on out,"

Friend, "Well, I'm not sure I can make it."

"Oh, come on, try"

The lifeguard musing, *Yea, try, you idiot. If you don't make it, that kid on the perch will save you.*

I'm sure all lifeguards through time and at all swimming areas are told endlessly, "Want to know how I learned to swim? My dad, uncle, cousin just picked me up and threw me in and said 'swim to shore.' And I did." If you are one of those story tellers, knock it off. If that were believable, why have lifeguards?

Before and during his teen years, Byron did so like to build and experiment. In fact, that mentality was what led him to his life's work as an electrical engineer. Once he was dabbling with something that involved electricity. In order to validate his experiment, he handed Molly a pair of pliers and told her to hold it to some object. She did and was knocked hard backward into a wall by a severe electrical jolt. When he asked for assistance with his inventions, it behooved a person to make inquiries. He could become completely absorbed in his experiments.

We had a Gravely self-propelled tractor used for mowing. Byron managed to devise an attachment to it to spray DDT to keep down the mosquitoes down. He and Dad even bought the DDT spray in big drums. We certainly didn't know much about DDT at that time, though my niece, Kathy, remembers me hurrying her into the house when he sprayed.

One of his building projects I was most interested in, was a water slide for the swimmers. It was built on the end of the opposite dock across from the lifeguard perch. This was to give it extra height for the ride and drop off into the water. From the perch on the opposite dock, I watched the construction taking place over a period of time, looking forward to its completion; From my view-point it looked like a mighty, fine slide. I really was very pleased when he asked me to be the first to try it out. Well, it was a speedy ride, but the end of the slide was tipped a little high. I whizzed down, and hit an abrupt bottom that flew me upward and outward into the lake. It actually hurt my lower back. I had to make my way to shallow water to recover. He was concerned regarding its structure. He studied it for some time and did endeavor to correct it, but didn't succeed entirely. It was quite entertaining to sit on the lifeguard perch watching across the way at people going down that thing once, and come up out of the water with a bemused expression. Rarely did they go back down it for a second turn.

Eventually we acquired a long water slide, not homemade,

set up in the shallow water especially for young children. That, too could be problematic. Older guys just had to go down that thing forwards, backwards, or two at a time. Whatever impressed. Once when there was a group of boys outdoing one another on that slide. There were just a few swimmers that evening, so I was keeping an eye out on them, perhaps anticipating a problem. One chubby boy, climbed up the ladder and with considerable twisting and manipulation, stationed himself backwards at the top. I realized his intention was to do a back somersault down the slide. To his shock and my amusement, he got a little off center, landed astraddle the side of the slide and zoomed all the way belly down with his butt facing the lifeguard perch. At the foot of the slide, there he stood in waist-deep water, red face contorted in pain, clutching the front of his suit. His friends were howling. I didn't dare laugh. I had to pretend I hadn't seen a thing

In the fall before school started, the local high school football team stayed in the cabins and held fall football practice. These were my school mates, so it wasn't easy for me. Once some of the boys at the dock were using profanity. In Dad's view, a male was *not* to cuss in front of a female. Dad was nearby, overheard the bad language and remonstrated with the boys pointing out me, a girl within hearing distance. Embarrassed I'm sure, one boy got a little sassy. The next thing, Dad had the boy by the seat of his britches, hiked up on his tippy toes, bouncing hm as they walked across the beach. Dad was talking quietly to him all the while, convincing him that he must not cuss in front of women. That fatherly counsel probably stayed with him.

One fall, a football player faked a drowning. It was late in the evening and getting dark. The beach had been cleared, when a call of alarm got to us up at our house. Dad ordered me to get to the beach to oversee the situation. If it were a true alarm, a certified lifeguard should be down there. So I ran to the beach. There was a cluster of boys on the raft, so doing my best to look official, I set out in a rowboat to check out the raft. As I approached, I could see the supposed victim lying on his stomach eyeing me. He certainly did not look like he was in any danger. He was surrounded by a few boys, who had witnessed his supposed drowning and perhaps participated in the saving. The coach had swum out there and was hovering over the boy. To my utter dismay, he was stripped of *all* his clothing. Why? Was it in order to jump in and swim to the rescue of the boy? I still cannot imagine what possessed him, as it was ridiculously unnecessary. There I was a teenage girl in a boat, and here were boys my age and a naked, male adult. Reflecting back on this, the coach he was responsible for a group of minors, and was accountable to their parents. Any tales told later would need to portray the image of a responsible man making a valiant rescue. My perception of the situation, was that the unnecessary nudity, lessened his effectiveness as a he-man. A naked man on a

M DAWN DAYTON

raft cannot achieve he-man status. Underwear would have been more effective. To really be certain he was covering all basis, he brought the boy up to our porch for him to recover there on our day bed under my care. Dad whispered to me, "Dawn, that the boy is obviously homesick. Now he just needs your attention." Hah! He was sure not going to get it from me. I was quite mortified over the naked coach and this fake "emergency figure" on the day bed, was the cause of much discomfort. Football players didn't impress me and never would.

⌐∾

Now that I am an elderly person and have given up so many enjoyable activities. One activity, that an elderly one does not have to abandon, is swimming. You may want to hide the seersucker body, but once it is in the water, it works and feels just like it always did. A few years ago, I discovered a community center near me that has a free, indoor heated pool. What a find! Having painful arthritis in my back and hip, I need to keep my joints moving so I go regularly. Swimming is such a beneficial exercise with no strain or pain. There are a few elderly ones there besides myself, to even make it a pleasant social event. I feel so stimulated by this discovery, I leap in the pool like a child, rather than use the steps like the other elderly ladies. When I do, I hear shouts of, "Show Off!" So many older folks, either bystanders or standing in the shallow water, have voiced to me that they are terrified of the water, or their parents were scared for them to swim or there was no place to swim. Yet, they wished to they could swim. So one day, I said to such a one, "It's never too late to learn to swim." And that is true. She took me up on it. I found by talking to her, pointing out that, unless the ceiling fell in, she couldn't possibly drown there in the shallow end. I laid flat out on the water demonstrating that one really doesn't sink. In short order we had a swimmer, and she was so excited and so was I. I have since taught many more to swim and I love it. To think there are older folks, who have all their life watched others swim, and not believe it could also be something they could do. Every once in a while, someone comes in to the community center looking for the lady that will teach them to swim. I find success by convincing them that one does not automatically sink and drown.

Recently, a Muslim lady came to the pool with a grandchild. She waded in the pool fully clothed. The only skin exposed was her face and hands. She wanted to swim. *Oh, oh,* I thought. I thought immediately, *she'll sink.* She didn't understand English. As I usual did, I demonstrated taking a deep breath, lying in the water face down, and to my amazement, without hesitation, she copied me. I forgot my joints, and concentrated on helping her. In short order, she was moving through the water, with her head down, paddling with her shod feet—a fast learner! I don't know who was more thrilled. She came the next day, and indicated she wanted to float on her back like I did. She did just so. With the dripping wet, heavy clothing, she floated. I indicated that I was going to swim and left her for a little while. Coming back to that end of the pool, I found her still flat on her back with her eyes closed, pounds of wet clothing and scarf, floating about her. The new lifeguard was glancing at her nervously. She looked as if she were a person, who had fallen in and was done for. We did not share a language, but I understood her big hug.

SCHOOLING IN TALLAHASSEE

B YRON, MOLLY AND I were in the local Leon High School in Tallahassee. Ronnie in middle school at the demonstration school at FSU. The school was about four miles out of the forest then eight miles east, Dad drove us out of the forest to the state road to catch a bus. Tallahassee was a hilly, small city, the seat of the state government with two major universities. I remember Tallahassee as a somewhat snobbish community, but at the same time had a genteel southern culture. That was the first time I had to mingle in a class-conscious mentality, but was not bothered by it. Because of the distance, we did not have much participation in extra-curricular activity. That was hard on Molly, who made friends easily, and wanted a social life.

While still new students at the high school, Molly was mortified to learn her brother, Byron, probably while deep into working out a mathematical formula, wondered into the girls' bathroom. Unperturbed he wondered back out. Then, in order to schedule subjects he needed later for college, he could not fit in the usual electives provided to male students, so he took a home economics class. All this Molly found to be detrimental to her longed-for popularity. She had a lot to say about it at home. She so longed for these things. She would walk through a room and suddenly leap into a high jump with arched back, in imitation of a longed for cheer leader role. Molly graduated at an early age, then took a few courses at FSU to get into nurses training and she was on her way. She did participate as a lifeguard and manned the concession stand, when she still was with us, although her heart wasn't in it.

One of the teachers at the high school was one dear named Mrs. Ritter. During the war, Mrs. Ritter, unknowingly had married a German spy. She lived, along with their two children in Europe. After the war the daughter wrote a book about the deprivations and bombing, they endured. The single mother had been quite heroic in trying to earn a living, while having to care for and protect her children. Once in America after the war, she became a teacher at our school, and her two children were students with me.

Each summer the county held a summer camp for the school children, with the teachers being the counselors. It ran for four weeks, each week bringing in a new batch of children. It was a very, well-run program. It was good not just for the kids, but gave the teachers a summer job as counselors. We really enjoyed serving them. it was fun getting to know our very own teachers outside the school setting. Mrs. Ritter was one of these teachers. We were all fond of her. She was a hefty lady, with enormous breasts. At swim period she would lounge in the shallow water, bobbing up and down. Those breasts resembled life buoys. There were sly comments by the hired help regarding those breasts; It couldn't be avoided.

One evening Byron was in his over-flow house, and heard loud screaming from the bathhouse close by. He raced down to find Mrs. Ritter in the doorway of the bath house. naked holding a towel over her body. She was screaming, "Snake! Snake!" Byron raced in and sure enough, there was a large rat snake wrapped around a shower faucet in the bathhouse with his head jutted out. Byron in a "saving the frightened lady" mode, made a rapid snatch and got it by its head. That snatch scared poor Mrs. Ritter so much, she dropped the towel and ran outside as is. He with the snake in one hand, grabbed her towel in the other, walked out, handed the towel to her, made sure she felt safe, and went back home, all in a day's work. That became a family story over time.

Years later at a class reunion, I was commiserating with that lady, about an unhappy marriage. In a firm voice she told me, "You must just persevere, my dear, just persevere." She knew what she was talking about. She certainly had shown perseverance during a horrendous time in wartime Europe, but was outdone by a harmless snake in Florida.

I confess to having awful handwriting. It may be because the brain goes faster than the pen. It could have been the inadequacy of that toilet paper used to learn cursive at the one-room school house. In school we wrote, then rewrote papers. I, and probably many others, have callouses on my middle finger from all the writing. We often had to take an essay test in high school. Once a teacher, Ms. Scarborough returned a paper, took me aside and whispered, "Dawn, my dear, I think you might could become a writer, but no one will be able to read it." She also whispered, that though I had good grades and sang in the chorus, I couldn't be invited into the honor society. It was that self-control problem, again. I am not sure that my inability to control my laughter would keep me out of the honor society today.

In the ninth grade I had a very strange woman, Latin teacher. Her class room was in a remote area on the third floor of the school that sat high on a hill. Her demeanor was almost menacing. She also exuded a rather sexual bearing, highly unusual for that time and place. She was whispered about and a there was feeling of discomfort among the boys. There was never a smile or word of commendation from her. The class atmosphere was tense, but we did learn Latin. In hot weather there in Florida, the windows were kept wide open. Sitting next to a window, I would put my Latin textbook on the window sill. I'm not sure what inspired it, but during class one day, I impulsively threw my Latin book out the window. I guess it was a show of bravery to rouse my stifled classmates. There was a deathly silence. The intimidating teacher with clenched lips, ordered me to go down and get the book. That was all it took; her look and voice, and I too was back into submission for the rest of the year and the year following.

M DAWN DAYTON

One more teacher I'll mention. . . a real charmer. In 1954 my senior year in high school, the Supreme Court made its historic decision, and President Eisenhower announced it to the nation. It was the end of school segregation. Like in Indiana, there were no black or brown faces at our schools, pools, restaurants, all that just absent from our world. This announcement was momentous! The morning following, my prim, proper English teacher, an old-school, Tallahassee girl, entered our classroom so angry she was trembling. She slammed a book on her desk and groused, "I am not going to teach niggers!"

Oh my. Smarty pants, I, raised my hand and said, "Oh, Mrs. Eustis, rest assured the magnolia trees will keep blooming in spite of this calamity."

She said, "Dawn, Leave the room, now." She followed me out in the hall, then ordered me to go straight to the principal's office. Very uneasy, down I went and told him the story and my role in it. He sat quietly looking sad, then thoughtfully said to me, "Dawn, your feelings are in the right place. Unfortunately, I can't do anything to defend you. More than that, she'll probably give you a lower grade." I was glad he warned me, because she did. But his comments were enough for me to simply ignore her after that. His empathy was enough.

Actually it took a lot longer after that for the schools to be integrated. A lot of private schools sprang up following that decree. As years went by, the adults were still adjusting, but the children were quicker to accept the matter. By the time my children were in school in the eighties, there were pockets of problems and will always be, unfortunately.

During my time at FSU, Martin Luther King was demonstrating. A lot of the FSU students were involved in the Civil Rights Movement. My history professor, told us that one of the janitors on our campus was a professor at the A&M University across town, but wasn't paid enough to live on, so was pushing a broom at our library. Gradually after the movement, it seemed to me that there was much improvement. It sickens me to sense and know that racism and its ugliness is alive and out front again.

The problem for me at school, was for laughing and causing distraction. No doubt, I was obnoxious. My close friend, Lecky, my side-kick, who also was a cut up, got me in a lot of mischief. I don't know how we discovered each other, but it was early after our arrival to Silver Lake. She loved Silver Lake and joined our Life Guard certification course and worked during the summers with us. She had polio in her early years and was left with a bad back. I think as a result of that polio, her family brought her a jeep to be certain she had her own transportation and would not be restricted. I was so impressed by a girl peer, zipping around in a red jeep. It was a wonderful friendship and has lasted to this day. She loved to swim, fish and to laugh. He folks owned a beach house on

Alligator Point down at the coast, as we called it. Then it was "going to the coast."

Looking back it was that all she had to do was look at me during class and I would start to laugh and couldn't control it. We would laugh until tears rolled down our faces. That simply wasn't done in the 1950s. Invariably I got sent to the library for it and it kept me out of the honor society. Surely teen-age girls today have a friend that can send them into peals of laughter. In the senior class yearbook I was voted the wittiest and I'm pictured sitting on a child-sized tractor in the yard of the governor's mansion. Why, there, I don't know. To the teachers who put up with me, witty really wasn't the correct word. I do love it even now to have someone say something that laughter squeezes out no matter how hard I try to control it. I truly liked school and feel I got to go to good public schools.

LIVING WITH VARMINTS

WORKING WITH THE public is never boring. The same goes for varmints. One snake that we did not fear, was a big one we called an oak snake. Oak snakes were large, harmless, and were the same color as Spanish moss in the oak trees, where they liked to exist in. I am careful not to say *hide,* as that would suggest they had intentions and made decisions. There are people who seem to think that snakes lurk up in trees, waiting to jump out to attack them. Wrong. Sometime they may *fall* out of a tree when startled.

One of my daughters, Nancy, had a boyfriend, who originated in Indiana. He was such a sissy. We took him canoeing in a quiet shaded stream, and the whole time we were out, his head was craned back looking up. It got on my nerves, so I finally said, "Gary, what are you looking for?"

A meek voice replied, "Are there snakes up in these trees? Could one jump out."

I'm thinking, *What's with this pitiful male creature?*

I said, "Get a grip, boy. You're in safe hands."

Once, when I was lifeguarding, I heard loud screaming and saw people running in all directions. A huge oak snake had fallen from an oak tree onto their picnic table. I'm sure a big snake, lying across the potato salad, was disconcerting.

That meant the snake had to be removed out of the vicinity and the folks reassured. Not that day, perhaps, but later those picnickers had a story to tell and could laugh about. In the telling amongst us, it was so funny. We always hoped to remove a snake rather than kill them and that should be true today.

Water snakes are not funny. There is a nonpoisonous one in southern states, that can be mean, if annoyed, and it is not timid. The water moccasin, sometimes called a Cottonmouth, is poisonous, and mean. We had both. We had to watch for them around the docks, while people were swimming.

While Byron was working on his deluxe water slide, he saw a large poisonous water moccasin come out from under the dock and head into the swimming area. It called for quick action. He let fly with a hammer he was holding, hoping to scare it off, and hit the thing right in the head and killed it. He brags about that. While in a row boat poling through the swampy area between lakes, he was having difficulty getting the boat between the trees and cypress knees. When it bumped up against a cypress tree, and a large water moccasin fell into the row boat. That entailed some action. He beat it to death with the oar.

Dad was walking home one night, and walked onto the porch, dragging a little pigmy rattlesnake behind him. Pigmy rattlers are about twelve to eighteen inches long, rather cute compared to a regular rattle snake that can get quite large. However, the Pigmies, though small, are very venomous.

Unbeknownst to Dad he walked by the snake that struck him, and got its fangs stuck in his pants leg, so he dragged it home and into the house.

Ronnie, barefoot, came up the same path one night, stepped on a snake and got bit. He hollered for someone to bring him a flashlight—Quick! That was a very serious request, because he needed to determine if the snake was poisonous. Dear Granny was on the porch with a flashlight. She hollers right back, "You're not getting my flashlight, young man. You didn't return it the last time."

One of Ronnie's girlfriends was in her car coming to the lake and realized she had seen a very large rattlesnake outside her car window, so she stopped and backed up over it to kill it, then put it into the trunk of the car. It was so long, she and the snake appeared in the Tallahassee Democrat. That would be illegal today. I went on-line to verify this last statement and in **vetsexplainspets.com** I found:

There are several interesting trends related to the topic of killing rattlesnakes in Florida. One trend is the increasing awareness of the importance of rattlesnakes in the ecosystem. As more people become educated about the role rattlesnakes play in controlling rodent populations, there is a growing appreciation for these reptiles.

Another trend is the rise of rattlesnake relocation services in Florida. Instead of killing rattlesnakes, many residents are opting to call in professionals to safely capture and relocate the snakes to a more suitable habitat. This trend reflects a shift towards more humane methods of dealing with wildlife encounters.

Even Mother had a nasty encounter with a snake. She went to open the concession stand door one morning. She noticed what looked like a rope wrapped around the door handle. It was peculiar and gave her pause, but she needed to get in, so she took ahold of the "rope" and it took offence and bit her. It was another rat snake.

In Apalachicola National Forest there are about forty-one different species of snakes. We were bound to have encounters with them. The dangerous ones wouldn't fall out of trees or wrap around a door handle. I could write a great deal about peoples' varying response to snakes. Mainly, if they do encounter one, it is to exaggerate its size or danger. Actually, fear and ignorance does get snakes needlessly killed. Just having a knowledge of the few venomous ones in an area, can ease much of the fear. In that area of Florida are three different rattle snakes, water moccasins, coral snakes and in some counties, copperheads. It is wise to be cautious. We are not their prey so there would not be any aggression on the part of these snakes. Harmless snakes can be a benefit to a homeowner. I have always believed that, yet now when I see videos and pictures of those Burmese Pythons in the Everglades, I react with fear and revulsion, but they don't belong there.

We aren't usually squeamish about something we know and understand, but even with that, I don't understand the need to make pets out of a non-native snake that can get twenty feet long, then release it or allow it to get loose to disrupt the ecology. Florida is being damaged by those snakes and other creatures released in neighborhoods and streams. I pontificate about these creatures too dumb to be pets, but having recently learned about the wonders of the octopus, makes me think twice about using the word dumb in relation to any living creature.

One afternoon I was putting on my bathing suit when it felt like a hammer blow to my upper thigh. I screeched, and to dad's amusement, ran through the house screaming. It was a scorpion bite. It didn't feel like a sting at all, but it sure hurt. I got another scorpion bite from one that was in bed with me. I even had a Florida palmetto bug crawl in my mouth while I was asleep, which woke me up. Oh, it was horrific! They are big, brown, insects. Nasty. You can hear them crunch when squashed. After that experience, I've remained so repelled by them, I gag on sight.

Another Florida bug is the big old rhinoceros beetle— they

look awful, but are not. I put one up near the face of a girlfriend one day and she retaliated by socking me in the face. It came to blows. The preacher of one of the church camps there broke it up. Mother wasn't as tolerant as Dad about fighting. She was furious at me, rightfully so.

When a suspected nuisance alligator needed to be removed from the lake, a Florida "cracker" from outside the park was called. The gator hunter went out into the lake with a large light and made alligator-like grunting noises. When the light catches the Gator's eyes they show vividly. Sure enough, he captured one and got it up as far as our cabin when it escaped. Our cabin was on concrete blocks as were all the cabins. This left crawl space where the gator ran to hide—under it went. Byron then was dispatched to solve this problem. He crawled on his belly under the house and there the gator was doing pushups and hissing. He started scooting back out and hollered, "Mama, get me Dad's gun." She did so. He crawled back under to face the gator, took aim and **click...**

Byron, "Mom, this thing is not loaded!"

Mom, "Of course not, Byron. Do you think I'd keep a loaded gun in the house?"

One morning, Ronnie was calling for us to come over to the other overflow cabin. He had something to show us, but we must go to him. He was lying in bed, with his arms above his head and in his hairy armpit was a litter of teeny, newborn mice. I could not make that up.

M DAWN DAYTON

One morning Mother woke up to discover a mouse running about on her dresser with a baby mouse in her mouth. It was a mother attempting to hide her babies behind things on the dresser. Dad was all set to kill the mouse, but Mother protested, touched by her heroic effort to save her babies. She wouldn't stand for it. Dad just shrugged and walked off.

One of my favorite little Florida varmints are the little grey chameleons. They loved our front porch, inside and outside. I spent an afternoon once entertaining Dad by tying a thin string behind their head and safety pinning a number of them to the screen. I named them after the Presidents of the US. Dad helped me naming them. It seems cruel to me now, though they ran around playfully. I'm sure I released them. The males had a little red and white flap that comes out of their neck. It's so cute. I assumed it was to attract the ladies. People that are scared of them, fear a bite, but the ones I played with, did not have teeth, just a bone ridge for holding on. To show a squeamish girl once that they don't bite, I held it up to my nose and it clamped on. I felt a tight pinch. I swayed my head around and it dangled, but did not let loose. She laughed hysterically at the sight, but still wouldn't even touch it.

Almost extinct now, are the pretty, little green snakes, that are harmless. If one appeared within grabbing distance we caught it. It was a perfect snake to offer to a person who were terrified of snakes, in order to convince them that snakes are not repellent and can be quite inoffensive. I'm sure these didn't have teeth either, and they are so docile they don't even attempt to bite in self-defense. The same goes for a hognose snake, and a garter snake to name a few. I truly don't understand people's fear of these harmless critters.

In the lake were big, ugly soft-shelled turtles and snapping The only time we saw them was when we caught one accidently while fishing. It could be a real problem to get the hook out to release it back in the water. Those guy's necks stretch as long as their bodies, and they can be vicious trying protect themselves. I once saw female soft shell come up out of the water to dig in the sand to lay her eggs, just like a sea turtle. Other swimmers there, were equally fascinated. A young man approached with an umbrella to hold over her to make her more comfortable.

GROWING UP

I WAS RATHER OLD before I got interested in boys. I can't say the same for Molly. I was sure she had more than one boy interested in her at the same time and could arrange things so she could enjoy the attention from all. While I was in the water and off the diving boards every chance I got, Molly would be decked out in swimsuit smeared with baby oil and lying on a towel sunbathing. If a goodlooking guy came near the beach, without seeming to be aware, she would arise to meander up on the high diving board and perform a perfect jack knife or swan dive much better than I ever could. When she was supposed to relieve me on the lifeguard perch, she was invariably late or not come at all.

One chore we all had in house work was two of us on dirty dishes duty with one washing and one drying. There was a little period of time during our early teens, when Molly presented me with a new, repugnant trick. It didn't last long. If she was the dishwasher, and I drying, and she would suddenly snatch the slopping, wet dishcloth out of the water and slap it across my face. It would cause absolute rage to boil up. She got away with that a few times. She tried that trick on Byron one day, when he was the dish dryer, and instantly realized the peril it put her in. Like lightening, she dashed for the door, made it through and slammed it shut, just before Byron threw the handful of eating utensils he was drying. They hit the door and then floor with a loud clatter. It ended that stunt.

The odd thing about this is our parents did not display anger or even arguments with each other. Nor do I remember my having problems with my brothers or they with one another. I'm not sure what Molly and I's problem may be have been other than, I was the baby born after she. She unexpectantly would hit me or in a crowd humiliate me. That was during our childhood, and she of course, had another story to tell. Whatever, we weren't close. I'm thankful, though, we could enjoy each other as adults. She could be so funny, telling stories involving her nursing duties or parenting at her own expense.

⸏

The big mess hall at Silver Lake was great for parties. Many of the sororities and fraternities from FSU wanted to have parties out there, probably to get away from campus scrutiny that curtailed drinking and sexual activity. Dad ran a trim ship, though. The university and Dad were in cahoots regarding their motives for going into the deep woods to party. He patrolled and kept a firm watch on their activities.

Then there was a Sea Scout party at the mess hall. A major event in my life. Molly had a date to attend that party and insisted that I be a date with her boyfriend's friend. I was about thirteen years old. I was upset at the very idea. I protested, but I lost to her persistence and Mother sided with her.

Here's what happened:

The event was in the fall, just before school started. Mother had made for me a new dirndl skirt, and I had a new blouse and saddle oxfords with white bobby socks—All set for the first day of school. I didn't like to wear shoes even to school, but shoes were necessary and Saddle oxfords were a must. To accompany my "date" I was expected to wear my new school clothes. I absolutely didn't want a date. I was sure I didn't know how to have a date. Molly told me to just do whatever the boy wanted to do. Huh? The boy's name was JP. How could I ever forget that name? His later behavior, indicated, that perhaps he too had an older sibling counseling him.

At the party JP and I stood together in somewhat unfriendly silence. Me, wondering, how I was to endure the evening. Finally after minutes of misery. he turned to me and said, "You want to go down to the lake?"

With that, things began to look up. I answered eagerly, "Want to canoe?"

He mumbled, "OK, I'm not sure, I know how."

I exclaimed, "And you're a *Sea* Scout?*" Sea said water, and water was synonymous with boats. And he a sea scout?*

It *was pitch dark. All the better. Out on the dark lake in a canoe! What fun.*

We got down to where the canoes were; It was muddy. What about my school saddle oxfords and white socks? If this had been any other occasion, rather than a canoe ride, I might have figured it was a no go. I grabbed the paddle and said decisively, "I get the stern." I took canoeing very seriously, and wasn't one to let just anyone man the stern. Making sure I got the stern required that I often would make haste to wade into the shallow water and slide into the canoe to kneel. I had that skill down pat, but this time, having a skirt and saddle oxfords on gave me some hesitation. There was only one thing to do. Get him settled with his back to me, then remove the saddle oxfords on the dock, and count on my skill in sliding in. Would my skirt get wet? Yes. It took some maneuvering to get the canoe in place next to the deck, so I could remove my shoes, get in. I was feeling rather smug with all of it, because I was getting the idea of a "date" out of my mind and doing my kind of fun. I shoved off. We shot pass the dock, when out of the blue I hear him say, "I'm ready to go back to the party now."

"What? We just got out here, for heaven's sake."

He mumbled, "I want go back to the party."

Remembering Molly's instruction, I reluctantly returned to the dock taking care to retrieve my saddle oxfords and white socks. As we made our way back up to the mess hall, JP abruptly grabbed me by the shoulders, pushed me down on a nearby bench, and pressed his mouth down on mine, hard.

He wiggled his head around, and I could feel his little buck teeth. I was positively alarmed and mortified. With my heart pounding, I leapt up. Attempting dignity, I brushed at my skirt and stated, "JP, I've got to tell my mother something." and marched briskly up to the mess hall with JP trailing. Mother was at the party, as a chaperone, fortunately for me. I went swiftly to her and said, "Mama, come with me right now!" I have something to tell you." In a manic state, I was half running for one of our over-flow houses, with her trying to keep up. Once there I climbed up on a bunk and began to cry, hysterically. I could hardly get my breath.

Mother must have put two and two together so, she pleaded, "Oh, Dawnie, what did he do?"

I screamed, "Mama, he kissed me!"

"Is that all, Dawnie?"

"Of course, that's all. What else *could* he do?"

She was relieved, I'm sure. I truly was shattered.

Then I begged her not to tell anyone. I had Molly in mind, who would have teased me and broadcasts it to all her friends. I didn't go back to the party.

Like Molly, Ronnie, was a lover boy, and was quite successful with the opposite sex. Once, when he was in high school, I saw one of our teachers kissing him under the water right below the life guard perch. Heavenly days! My girlfriends all loved him. He joined my slumber parties, in the cabins. He would rub backs and I would hear him in whispered conversations. He went through quite a few women in life and broke hearts.

One fall, I was having a slumber party in a cabin full of my friends from school. The grounds were empty of public, so I got the bright idea that we could all go skinny dipping in the lake close by. It was dare, and all were game. Down at the water, we were jumping off the high diving board. It can be truly scary in the dark, to look down at black water and jump into it. One girl was on the board and we were chanting, "Jump, Jump," while all the while she was swinging her arms, but couldn't get the nerve up to jump. We were losing patience—All of the sudden all the beach lights switched on, and she sure jumped. We could hear Dad laughing from way back at the beach light-switch in the concession stand.

One time Mother decided to give me a home permanent. My hair was straight with no body and I didn't like to primp. Home perms at that time were prone to damage hair, unless the giver timed the procedure very carefully. That time, when all rollers were in place, she saturated the curls with the harsh chemical provided. To our dismay, we discovered we had no running water coming into the house, right at the precise time to rinse the lotion out. So Mother, cried, "Quick, Dawn, go jump in the lake!" Fully clothed with a head full of curlers, I ran like mad though the trees, down past the concession stand, down the hill across the dock and dived in. It saved my hair.

Mother was concerned whether Ronnie and I would ever become truly civilized; At Silver Lake there were few opportunities for culture. There was an occasion, when the senior students from the Leon High School were invited to the DuPont mansion for a formal ball. To write this, I had to go on-line to query the actuality of the "DuPonts" in Tallahassee as my memory of it is quite vague. Tallahassee had a number of historic, beautiful, old antebellum mansions. (From Wikipedia: One was the Southwood Plantation bought for the DuPont estate in the 1940s.) So it must have been true. The invitations must have been a kind of gesture toward the community. Who knows? If they were inviting the Tallahassee 'nobles', I wouldn't have received an invitation. Having to purchase and wear a formal dress—Heaven forbid—And making an appearance at a ball. It was a time of great anxiety on my part what with the formal dress, strapless bra, and mascara. Before my departure from home, Mother was frantic that I was going to catch my dress on fire by brushing against our only heater, a kerosine one, in the tiny hallway of our little house.

While there, one of the teenage DuPont youths at that party asked me to dance. That made me more nervous. After the dance, he very politely invited me to take a tour of their mansion. I was agreeable, but in my mind, I was thinking that if he only knew--- *I just departed a four room little abode in the middle of the Apalachicola National Forest*; I could have shown him a novel thing or two, back in our forest. He chose to show me their great trophy room. Off the walls hung the dead carcasses of large animals hunted, killed and stuffed. I, who loved wildlife and all kinds of varmints, was fairly horrified. I do not think I was so crass to express my jumbled feelings about the sight. That ball and later the senior prom was the only time I had to dress for any occasion during my teen years.

$$\backsim$$

At various times at the lake, there would be campers that just enjoy the outdoors and solitude, and would stay for weeks. One early fall, there was such a man, perhaps in his thirties. He wore shorts with rather odd-looking sandals, I called them his "Jesus sandals" because he said he had toured Jerusalem once in those sandals. He was reserved, but warm and friendly to us all. He told us he was the grandson of T. S. Elliot, the poet. There was nothing about him that suggested we might doubt him. I was writing a term paper at the time; he helped me with it and I got a good grade. Mother happened to be painting a mural in the mess hall for the forest service at that time,and he expressed interest in her work. She was playing classical music, and he was versed in that. He would roam around the lake and into the woods. I had to drive him to the FSU campus once, because he was applying for a job there. He left when it got too chilly for roughing it. As I write this, like the DuPonts I wonder, *if that's who he was, and how did T. S. Elliott's grandson ever happen to come to remote Silver Lake? Just maybe my memory is faulty,* so I went on-line again and learned that T S Eliot, though married twice, never had children. The *grandson* was a fake. Or perhaps, old T S, the poet, was guilty of untold hanky-panky.

∽

Back then, people who camped and enjoyed the outdoors, were on the whole good people. We rarely had serious problems with trouble makers or drunks. During the summer, it would really have us busy, covering swimming, concession, cleaning bathhouses, picking up picnic trash. It was twelve-hour days, seven days a week. Some of our teenage friends who loved being at the lake, were hired on. Dad himself was very service minded, and we knew to be pleasant even when stretched to the limit or tired. People truly liked Dad. He could be very humorous and had a natural talent for public relations.

We did have occasional disagreeable incidents. One, such was with one particular church camp. This one group that came every year would lease all the cabins, facilities and mess hall. That would mean that in addition to the that group of cabin campers, the grounds also had the regular day use swimmers and the picnickers along with tent campers. When camp was·that full, Dad was liable to chant, "All right, it's all hands-on deck now."

There was this one little, red headed preacher with one particular group that leased all the cabins and mess hall for church camp. He bustled about giving orders, and somehow just rubbed Dad wrong. This group also created a bit of vandalism. There was a broken toilet once in the camper's bathhouse. The man denied it was his group's doing. We knew otherwise. He had a sense of entitlement that didn't set well at Silver Lake, as he demanded services he thought below him.

One evening Dad came home fuming, muttering threats. His charming personality was not evident. He announced, "Peggy, so help me, I'm going to nail that *#&**, little Caesar to the cross!"

And Peggy, "Oh, Hansel, not in front of the children." We heard those words so often.

When cabins were full, it was arranged for the milk and bread delivery trucks that serviced the cabin campers, to come up to the main gate in the early morning and honk their horns for the gate to be unlocked. The responsible camp leader would then have a little early morning walk up to the locked gate to let them in to deliver their food items.

One morning before daylight, a horn starting honking close by our house and didn't stop. Little Caesar, the designated gate opener, associated the horn to be the bread or milk truck at the gate. He foggily arose and began the walk up there to let them in. Ronnie also got up to hunt down the source of the horn. Earlier in the evening, a car with a few young men came in and were prepared to spend the night in their car, so they went to an overflow spot, practically in our front yard. It happened the young men were deaf. One of them sleeping in the front seat had turned over, laid his foot in the steering wheel and thus the horn. It awakened little Caesar and over hundred other people, mostly children in the cabins.

⤸

In the small towns along the panhandle of Florida there was such poverty. There was money all along the coast with the beaches and tourists, however some of the rural folks inland barely made a living and lived in shanties. There was one young man, who drove an old, old truck. It didn't have much of a floor in the cabin, and the back was held together with rattly boards. Mom was very friendly with him, so he would drive out with his girlfriend just to chat with her. Both, wore dirty, clothes and were barefoot. Their courtship was real. They would make eye contact with each other and giggle. Mother was touched.

About to pass by her shanty one day, I stopped to chat with her. She was sorting and boxing earth worms for fishing, to be sold at a little local store. She probably would make only a few cents.

After the couple got married, she got pregnant and they came out to share that happy news with Mother. During a visit, Mother got rather troubled regarding her ignorance about the pregnancy and her baby's health. As she had done often through the years, she again had a person to help. She arranged to have her seen by our physician, a very gentle, southern gentleman. The day of the appointment, Mother had her take a shower and groomed her. After the exam, the doctor gently told Mother he suspected the lady was consumed with worms.

Then there came a day they came to show off their babies, twins, with Mother. The babies were in a cardboard box, and each was sucking a baby bottle, that contained a dark liquid. Mother inquired about the contents of the bottles and was informed it was Pepsi-Cola. It may seem I am poking fun, but if that were true, it would have to be for a soft chuckle mingled with a load of compassion. I have known many, many clean persons, in sharp clothes, even wearing shoes, that were putrid trash. This didn't apply with these two.

All the adventuresome, fun-filled, hardworking hours, happened from late spring through the early fall months. The rest of the months were very pleasant as well, and so peaceful. Each night we slept to the song of a whippoorwill, frogs and bugs. We had adapted quite well to our camping style cabin. We were surrounded by big trees and, and wildlife The two lakes were close enough to see and walk to. Ronnie and

M DAWN DAYTON

Molly might have been restless. Mother and I were content. The environment was conducive to good study habits, so we did well in school. I loved to read, so we always kept a supply of books on hand. One by one we grew up and went are own way.

We grew up secure knowing that our parents loved each other, loved us and were fun and good people. Yet they were flawed as we all are. I think Mother did not want to use physical punishment. Kids, being kids and we were a rambunctious bunch, must have been a challenge. We had a lot of freedom to be ourselves. Even if I was hyperactive, I don't remember that I was singled out for punishment at all. What I do remember is that I was shamed. Perhaps it was to teach me compassion. If were complain to Mother about a difficulty or disagreement with another person, whether it was a sibling or outside the family, she would say to me, "Dawnie, what did you do to make him or her want to retaliate?" Somehow, I was made to feel guilty about any disagreement, my fault or not.

From the way Granny interacted with us kids. I'm sure she was a harsh mother. Mother then, had to have issues that manifested itself with how she dealt with us. Discipline is generational. I hasten to say, Mother was never harsh. Looking back, I believe that Mother might have had some depression problems, as well. That would not be voiced or mentioned. After all, she had lost Dad when she was still in her forties. She told me once that Granny used to sleep when she was depressed. That information let me know there are probably depression genes floating around. Anyway, depression runs in our family then and now. I can be consumed by guilt. In middle age I had to be hospitalized for depression and anxieties for a short time. My sister, Molly had to, as well.

One sunny, pleasant day in Brown County I was out in our yard with a mother cat and her newborn kittens. She was a very calm mother cat and allowed us to play with her babies early on after their birth. I was very touched by the babies nursing their mother, their little paws pressing her abdomen. Curious, I picked up a kitten and pulled up my T-shirt to see if it would attach to my nipple. I wasn't being sneaky about it. All the sudden out of nowhere, my peace was shattered by a braying voice, "I see you, you naughty, dirty little girl. Just what do you think you're doing? You bad girl." It was Granny. Remembering the confusion and shame has lasted me eighty years, although I did manage to nurse my babies quite efficiently and happily.

In some ways, we kids were very responsible. We were associating with and serving such a broad, strata of individuals. We delight in meeting new and interesting people, and find it easy to establish rapport with individuals of all sorts. It is somewhat powerful to look into an acquaintance's eyes, and sense you have seen beyond the surface appearance. Yet, we had been so sheltered in other ways. Our father had good jobs during the depression and war time, and we were healthy.

Death had not touched our family, until our father died. It was such a good childhood.

We all love laughter. I'm so thankful for the Mead sense of humor. To be able to see humor in ourselves as well as others is a gift. Typical of so many depressives, all of us are considered witty. I can take a happening that was horrible when it came about, but turn it into a humorous story to tell. It lightens the load. There are occasions when I realize that a person is laughing at something I've said, and I'm puzzled, because I feel rotten.

There are many, many stories of comedians and artists who commit suicide; Red Skeleton, Robin Williams, singer, Naomi Judd to name a few. I hear of a suicide, and it jumps into my mind to wonder how long they walked around deeply depressed all the time cracking people up with wit or impressing others with a talent, then finally thinking to themselves, "I can't go on with this any longer." I'm so thankful to be living in a time when depression is better understood and there is help, though even then it is not always enough.

Mom was not demonstrative by nature, but Dad was. My friends would run and hug him when they came to visit. I watched one day, he was on the couch, prone, with one of his first granddaughters on his chest. She was looking down with her drool running on his face, while he softly talked with her. Occasionally, when we were together with him and Mother, he would throw his arms around her and say, "You know what your mom used to say to me? "Treat me rough, treat me tough, I kind of like that cave man stuff."

Then she, obviously embarrassed would say, "Oh, Hansel, not in front of the children."

Our house was so small we had to take pains for privacy. Conversations were so easily overheard. Mother, who was so modest, when changing clothes would to try conceal herself by backing against the clothes in her closet, using the door as a shield. I could hear from their bedroom Dad, in a falsetto voice, say, "Oh, Peggy, I see a bit of flesh."

That followed by, "Oh, Hansel, not in front of the children."

I was awakened one night, by Dad declaring he had swallowed his false teeth. After much searching with Mother reassuring him, his uppers were discovered stuck to the back of his pajama top by the adhesive that kept them in his mouth. He told her, "Something was hurting my back, but I couldn't think what it could be."

With another awakening, I was jolted up to sounds of distress from mother claiming she had been hit in the head and was bleeding. With all the lights turned on, I came in to see her hands in her hair, which was blobbed up with a sticky matter that felt like blood and she assumed it was. After an examination, though, we realized that Dad had hidden a Hershey bar under his pillow, that had slipped out and in the Florida heat, and had melted. She had managed to lay her head in it.

He did need to watch his weight, so Mother would mildly fuss at him if he got up in the night to raid the refrigerator. This actually took place every night. One night, he answered her back, "Now Peggy, surely you realize the amount of pleasure this refrigerator has given me? Why, I'd like to be buried in this refrigerator, if you will be so kind."

Silver Lake was a success story. When we arrived it was a desolate spot in a vast national forest. Our father and mother must have seen all the potential and inspired us as a family to work together to make it happen. And what an experience it was: as long-running adventure. What I said at the beginning of this story, is true. We did not think of it as adventuresome. We were making a living, and it was our life style. One of the biggest gifts we received, is that we were not under the pressure of conformity. We were allowed to be ourselves and choose our future always with their support.

One other observation regarding my parents is that they were intelligent, deep people. We had in that camping cabin, a home with a father in baggy. khaki pants, a mother in pedal pushers—two intelligent, loving, integrity keepers in a class of their own. I never understood what other teens felt, when they complained about their parents. I took pride in mine. I looked forward my dad waiting for me at the bus stop, when the school bus brought me home. My friends from school came from the popular students. I expect some of my friendships, stemmed from the swimming, and slumber parties in the cabins. Pretty wild stuff for the 1950s, but Silver Lake was so secluded, there was really nothing wild about it. We knew that our parents were extra-special people worthy of our love and admiration. We never had reason to doubt that.

In some ways, we kids were very responsible. We were associating with and serving such a broad, strata of individuals. We enjoy in meeting new and interesting people, and find it easy to establish rapport with individuals of all sorts. It is somewhat powerful to look into an acquaintance's eyes, and sense you have seen beyond the surface appearance. Yet, we had been so sheltered in other ways. Our father had good jobs during the depression and war time, and we were healthy. Death had not touched our family, until our father died. With all the challenges, because of strong parenting and love, it was such a good childhood.

I only had my beloved father, nineteen years. He died in 1956 from a long-anticipated heart attack. Before that, we were very conscious that he was going downhill. Mother was taking on more of the work of running the park. Dad though did continue with the decision making, advising, and cooking for us, supporting us every way he could.

Byron was in the Navy, when Dad had one heart attack.

Then there was a final one. Molly had gone from home for nursing school, then marriage. That left Moher, Ronnie and myself to keep the park running. Some of our friends and a few others continued come out to work for us in the summer.

The night of dad's death, one of us related an amusing story involving him. Grief- stricken, we then sat up all that night relating tales of dad's humorous antics laughing and crying. Mother later told me that night had been such a comfort to her.

Mother hardly had time to grieve, because people continued to stream into the park. In 1955 Mother reported in the Tallahassee Democrat, that there were 279 campers stayed in the camp. By August of her last year there was an impressive. 3,100 campers. That was not counting the day users. That was when there was only, she and Ronnie left to be "all hands on deck." I was there on their final day, and developed such a massive migraine, I could hardly walk. I just was sick about leaving the place.

When Byron completed a stint in the Navy, he returned to Tallahassee and Silver Lake, He was married and attended FSU at the same time I was there. He used an electronic engineering degree to become successful business man. Molly completed nurses training to become an RN, and was a compassionate nurse the rest of her life. She married an Air Force pilot and had four children. After Dad died, I sort of lost heart. I decided to take a semester off, instead dropped out with enough credits to be a senior. I got married, and had four children. Ronnie married, had three children and went into park work in Florida. Park work was all he had known, so he was a natural.

We had our dear mother for another thirty three years. She had a love for antiques, and after leaving Silver Lake, had her own antique business and was a respected antique appraiser in Tallahassee, Florida.

Hansel and Peggy Mead
1920's

From left Dawn, Byron Molly Mead
1930's

Our Granny, Theresa Schwartz
Born 1882

Molly and Dawn Mead
Typical pose

Life Magazine 1946 with article concerning the Disney lambs
Byron holding   Midnight   Molly in the corner

Vandal Hacks Off Part Of Bear's Tongue

"Friend Joe" probably won't be so friendly any more to visitors at Brown County State Park.

The 10-year-old black bear has learned his lesson about human beings the hard way. A vandal hacked off an inch of Joe's tongue.

Hansel Mead, superintendent of the park, said he would prefer that the tragedy of "Friend Joe" remain unpublicized. The act of cruelty occurred June 3 and came to light only yesterday.

Mead said keepers found Joe panic-stricken in his cage and an inch of his tongue lying outside the bars.

Now he is recovering, but he is on a diet of milk and milk-soaked dog biscuits.

State game wardens and state police were notified but so far no clews have led to the person who mutilated the pet bear.

Disney "cell" setup of original Pinochio film 1946

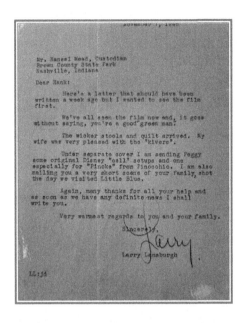

November 7, 1940

Mr. Hansel Mead, Custodian
Brown County State Park
Nashville, Indiana

Dear Hank:

Here's a letter that should have been
written a week ago but I wanted to see the film
first.

We've all seen the film now and, it goes
without saying, you're a good "green man."

The wicker stools and quilt arrived. My
wife was very pleased with the "kivers".

Under separate cover I am sending Peggy
some original Disney "cell" setups and one
especially for "Pinoke" from Pinocchio. I am also
mailing you a very short scene of your family, shot
the day we visited Little Blue.

Again, many thanks for all your help and
as soon as we have any definite news I shall
write you.

Very warmest regards to you and your family.

Sincerely,

Larry

Larry Lansburgh

LL:jd

Dawn at Juniper Springs in Florida
During Xmas holiday.
It was cold enough to wear a coat , but I had been swimming.
Note the saddle oxfords

Dawn and Molly with chosen lamb Midnight
Indianapolis Star 1946

Silver Lake in the heart of Apalachicola National Forest

Dressed up for square dance night in BCSP
Man with pipe Hansel Mead, our dad
Mead Girls: Molly left and Dawn far right

ABOUT DAWN DAYTON

D AWN HAS ALWAYS enjoyed being outdoors. Some have said she is independent and adventurous. When three of her four children were small, she organized a six-week road trip that went from Florida across the Southwest up thru California to Washington then home. It involved pulling a pop-up camper behind a van, camping all the way in National Parks and occasional private campgrounds or just the woods. That was her idea of a vacation . She camped with her children for a whole summer in Maine and another in the US Virgin Islands. While living in Florida and Tennessee the family frequently camped in the National forests and State Parks.

Her other great love is reading. While reading one book, she might have another stashed nearby, always making sure she has one available when she is finished with the current one. She reads a great variety of books some for entertainment, some for information and some to help her cope with life's trials. Wherever she has lived she has been a patron of the local library and thinks of them as a big source of enrichment to her life.

Also, throughout her life she has been an unfulfilled writer. While working in the marketing department at a local HCA hospital authored a monthly newsletter and another for a Seniors' organization the hospital sponsored. When humorous happenings of family life occurred, she put them in writing either in letters or just written for her own satisfaction. She has been told she is a good story teller, so after her brother produced a genealogy, she decided the family's stories needed to be recorded along with it. So after living nearly a century of life, she produced *"Roughing It"* wanting it to be an account of a very special childhood, rich with love and heartwarming, humorous experiences.

Now she swims regularly for relief from painful arthritis at a local community pool. She has found that she can help older people, who are fearful of swimming or have never learned, and can get them to swim. People approach her at a local Community center and request a swimming lesson.

She now lives outside Nashville, Tennessee, with her husband who is ninety-five years old, who was a NASA engineer, and only a domestic cat, nicknamed Kitty.

Printed in the United States
by Baker & Taylor Publisher Services